THE TRAVELLERS' LIBRARY

*

ANGELS AND MINISTERS

THE TRAVELLERS' LIBRARY

THE AUTOBIOGRAPHY OF A SUPER-TRAMP
by W. H. Davies

EARLHAM by Percy Lubbock

SELECTED PREJUDICES by H. L. Mencken

THE BLACK DOG by A. E. Coppard

WIDE SEAS AND MANY LANDS by Arthur Mason

CAN SUCH THINGS BE by Ambrose Bierce

BABBITT by Sinclair Lewis

THE CRAFT OF FICTION by Percy Lubbock

THE MIND IN THE MAKING by James Harvey Robinson

THE WAY OF ALL FLESH by Samuel Butler

EREWHON by Samuel Butler

EREWHON REVISITED by Samuel Butler

THE DREAM by H. G. Wells

ADAM AND EVE AND PINCH ME by A. E. Coppard

TWILIGHT IN ITALY by D. H. Lawrence

DOG AND DUCK by Arthur Machen

DUBLINERS by James Joyce

Uniform with this volume

ANGELS AND MINISTERS
AND OTHER VICTORIAN PLAYS

by

LAURENCE HOUSMAN

LONDON
JONATHAN CAPE 30 BEDFORD SQUARE

Angels and Ministers AND *Possession* WERE FIRST
PUBLISHED IN 1921 AND *Dethronements* IN 1922
REPRINTED IN TRAVELLERS' LIBRARY 1926

PRINTED IN GREAT BRITAIN

Introduction

THE Victorian era has ceased to be a thing of yesterday; it has become history; and the fixed look of age, no longer contemporary in character, which now grades the period, grades also the once living material which went to its making.

With this period of history those who were once participants in its life can deal more intimately and with more verisimilitude than can those whose literary outlook comes later. We can write of it as no sequent generation will find possible ; for we are bone of its bone and flesh of its flesh ; and when we go, something goes with us which will require for its reconstruction, not the natural piety of a returned native, such as I claim to be, but the cold, calculating art of literary excursionists whose domicile is elsewhere.

Some while ago, before Mr. Strachey had made the name of Victoria to resound as triumphantly as it does now, a friend asked why I should trouble to resuscitate these Victorian remains. My answer is because I myself am Victorian, and because the Victorianism to which I belong is now passing so rapidly into history, henceforth to present to the world a colder aspect than that which endears it to my own mind.

The bloom upon the grape only fully appears when it is ripe for death. Then, at a touch, it passes, delicate and evanescent as the frailest blossoms of spring. Just at this moment the Victorian age has that bloom upon it—autumnal, not spring-like—which, in the nature of things, cannot last. That bloom I have tried to illumine before time wipes it away.

Under this rose-shaded lamp of history, domestically designed, I would have these old characters look young again, or not at least as though they belonged to another age. This wick which I have kindled is short, and will not last ; but, so long as it does, it throws on them the commentary of a contemporary light. In another generation the bloom which it seeks to irradiate will be gone ; nor will anyone then be able to present them to us as they really were.

Contents

PART ONE: ANGELS AND MINISTERS

PAGE

I. THE QUEEN: GOD BLESS HER! . . . 15
    (A Scene from Home-Life in the Highlands)

II. HIS FAVOURITE FLOWER 47
    (A Political Myth Explained)

III. THE COMFORTER 63
    (A Political Finale)

PART TWO

IV. POSSESSION 89
    (A Peep-Show in Paradise)

PART THREE: DETHRONEMENTS

V. THE KING-MAKER 13
    (Brighton—October, 1891)

VI. THE MAN OF BUSINESS 35
    (Highbury—August, 1913)

VII. THE INSTRUMENT 71
    (Washington—March, 1921)

Part One

Angels and Ministers

The Queen:
God Bless Her!

Dramatis Personæ

QUEEN VICTORIA   LORD BEACONSFIELD

MR. JOHN BROWN   A FOOTMAN

The Queen : God Bless Her !

A Scene from Home-Life in the Highlands

The august Lady is sitting in a garden-tent on the lawn of Balmoral Castle. Her parasol leans beside her. Writing-materials are on the table before her, and a small fan, for it is hot weather ; also a dish of peaches. Sunlight suffuses the tent interior, softening the round contours of the face, and caressing pleasantly the small plump hand busy at letter-writing. The even flow of her penmanship is suddenly disturbed ; picking up her parasol, she indulgently beats some unseen object, lying concealed against her skirts.

QUEEN.   No : don't scratch ! Naughty ! Naughty !

> (*She then picks up a hand-bell, rings it, and continues her writing. Presently a fine figure of a man in Highland costume appears in the tent-door. He waits awhile, then speaks in the strong Doric of his native wilds.*)

MR. J. BROWN. Was your Majesty wanting anything, or were you ringing only for the fun?

> (*To this brusque delivery her Majesty responds with a cosy smile, for the special function of Mr. John Brown is not to be a courtier; and, knowing what is expected of him, he lives up to it.*)

QUEEN. Bring another chair, Brown. And take Mop with you: he wants his walk.

MR. J. B. What kind of a chair are you wanting, Ma'am? Is it to put your feet on?

QUEEN. No, no. It is to put a visitor on. Choose a nice one with a lean-back.

MR. J. B. With a lean back? Ho! Ye mean one that you can lean back in. What talk folk will bring with them from up south, to be sure! Yes, I'll get it for ye, Ma'am. Come, Mop, be a braw little wee mon, and tak' your walk!

> (*And while his Royal Mistress resumes her writing, taking Mop by his " lead," he prepares for departure.*)

Have ye seen the paper this morning yet? Ma'am.

> (*The address of respect is thrown in by way of afterthought, or, as it were, reluctantly. Having to be in character, his way is to tread heavily on the border-line which divides familiarity from respect.*)

QUEEN. Not yet.

MR. J. B. (*departing*). I'll bring it for ye, now.

QUEEN. You had better send it.

J. B. (*turning about*). What did ye say ? . . . Ma'am.

QUEEN. " Send it," Brown, I said. Mop mustn't be hurried. Take him round by the stables.

> (*He goes : and the Queen, with a soft, indulgent smile, that slowly flickers out as the labour of composition proceeds, resumes her writing.*)
>
> (*Presently* ENTERS *a liveried Footman, who stands at attention with the paper upon a salver. Touching the table at her side as an indication, the Queen continues to write. With gingerly reverence the man lays down the paper and goes. Twice she looks at it before taking it up ; then she unfolds it ; then lays it down, and takes out her glasses ; then begins reading. Evidently she comes on something she does not like ; she pats the table impatiently, then exclaims :*)

Most extraordinary !

> (*A wasp settles on the peaches.*)

And I wish one could kill all wicked pests as easily as you.

> *(She makes a dab with the paper-knife, the wasp escapes.)*

Most extraordinary!

> *(Relinquishing the pursuit of wasps, she resumes her reading.)*
>
> *(In a little while Mr. John Brown returns, both hands occupied. The chair he deposits by the tent door, and hitches Mop's " lead" to the back of that on which the Queen is sitting. With the small beginnings of a smile she lowers the paper, and looks at him and his accompaniments.)*

QUEEN. Well, Brown? Oh, yes; that's quite a nice one. . . . I'm sure there's a wasps' nest somewhere; there are so many of them about.

J. B. Eh, don't fash yourself! Wasps have a way of being aboot this time of year. It's the fruit they're after.

QUEEN. Yes: like Adam and Eve.

J. B. That's just it, Ma'am.

QUEEN. You'd better take it away, Brown, or cover it; it's too tempting.

J. B. *(removing the fruit)*. Ah! Now if God had only done that, maybe we'd still all be running aboot naked.

QUEEN. I'm glad He didn't, then.

18

J. B. Ye're right, Ma'am.

QUEEN. The Fall made the human race decent, even if it did no good otherwise. Brown, I've dropped my glasses.

(*He picks them up and returns them.*)

QUEEN. Thank you, Brown.

J. B. So you're expecting a visitor, ye say?

QUEEN. Yes. You haven't seen Lord Beaconsfield yet, I suppose?

J. B. Since he was to arrive off the train, you mean, Ma'am? No: he came early. He's in his room.

QUEEN. I hope they have given him a comfortable one.

J. B. It's the one I used to have. There's a good spring-bed in it, and a kettle-ring for the whisky.

QUEEN. Oh, that's all right, then.

J. B. Will he be staying for long? Ma'am.

QUEEN. Only for a week, I'm afraid. Why?

J. B. It's about the shooting I was thinking: whether it was the deer or the grouse he'd want to be after.

QUEEN. I don't think Lord Beaconsfield is a sportsman.

J. B. I know that, Ma'am, well enough. But there's many who are not sportsmen that think

B

they've got to do it—when they come north of the Tweed.

QUEEN. Lord Beaconsfield will not shoot, I'm sure. You remember him, Brown, being here before?

J. B. Eh! Many years ago, that was; he was no but Mr. Disraeli then. But he was the real thing, Ma'am: oh, a nice gentleman.

QUEEN. He is always very nice to me.

J. B. I remember now, when he first came, he put a tip into me hand. And when I let him know the liberty he had taken, "Well, Mr. Brown," he said, "I've made a mistake, but I don't take it back again!"

QUEEN. Very nice and sensible.

J. B. And indeed it was, Ma'am. Many a man would never have had the wit to leave well alone by just apologising for it. But there was an understandingness about him, that often you don't find. After that he always talked to me like an equal—just like yourself might do. But Lord, Ma'am, his ignorance, it was surprising!

QUEEN. Most extraordinary you should think that, Brown!

J. B. Ah! You haven't talked to him as I have, Ma'am: only about politics, and poetry, and things like that, where, maybe, he knows a bit more than I do (though he didn't know his Burns so well as a man ought that thinks to make laws for Scotland!).

But to hear him talking about natural facts, you'd think he was just inventing for to amuse himself! Do you know, Ma'am, he thought stags had white tails like rabbits, and that 'twas only when they wagged them so as to show, that you could shoot them. And he thought that you pulled a salmon out o' the water as soon as you'd hooked him. And he thought that a haggis was made of a sheep's head boiled in whisky. Oh, he's very innocent, Ma'am, if you get him where he's not expecting you.

QUEEN. Well, Brown, there are some things you can teach him, I don't doubt; and there are some things he can teach you. I'm sure he has taught me a great deal.

J. B. Ay? It's a credit to ye both, then.

QUEEN. He lets me think for myself, Brown; and that's what so many of my ministers would rather I didn't. They want me to be merely the receptacle of their own opinions. No, Brown, that's what we Stewarts are never going to do!

J. B. Nor would I, Ma'am, if I were in your shoes. But believe me, you can do more, being a mere woman, so to speak, than many a king can do.

QUEEN. Yes; being a woman has its advantages, I know.

J. B. For you can get round 'em, Ma'am; and you can put 'em off; and you can make it very awkward for them—very awkward—to have a difference of opinion with you.

QUEEN (*good-humouredly*). You and I have had differences of opinion sometimes, Brown.

J. B. True, Ma'am; that *has* happened; I've known it happen. And I've never regretted it, never! But the difference there is, Ma'am, that I'm not your Prime Minister. Had I been—you'd 'a been more stiff about giving in—naturally! Now there's Mr. Gladstone, Ma'am; I'm not denying he's a great man; but he's got too many ideas for my liking, far too many! I'm not against temperance any more than he is—put in its right place. But he's got that crazy notion of " local option " in his mind; he's coming to it, gradually. And he doesn't think how giving " local option," to them that don't take the wide view of things, may do harm to a locality. You must be wide in your views, else you do somebody an injustice.

QUEEN. Yes, Brown; and that is why I like being up in the hills, where the views *are* wide.

J. B. I put it this way, Ma'am. You come to a locality, and you find you can't get served as you are accustomed to be served. Well! you don't go there again, and you tell others not to go; and so the place gets a bad name. I've a brother who keeps an inn down at Aberlochy on the coach route, and he tells me that more than half his customers come from outside the locality.

QUEEN. Of course; naturally!

J. B. Well now, Ma'am, it'll be for the bad

locality to have half the custom that comes to it turned away, because of local option! And believe me, Ma'am, that's what it will come to. People living in it won't see till the shoe pinches them; and by that time my brother, and others like him, will have been ruined in their business.

QUEEN. Local option is not going to come yet, Brown.

J. B. (*firmly*). No, Ma'am, not while I vote conservative, it won't. But I was looking ahead; I was talking about Mr. Gladstone.

QUEEN. Mr. Gladstone has retired from politics. At least he is not going to take office again.

J. B. Don't you believe him, Ma'am. Mr. Gladstone is not a retiring character. He's in to-day's paper again—columns of him; have ye seen?

QUEEN. Yes; quite as much as I wish to see.

J. B. And there's something in what he says, I don't deny.

QUEEN. There's a great deal in what he says, I don't understand, and that I don't wish to.

J. B. Now you never said a truer thing than that in your life, Ma'am! That's just how I find him. Oh, but he's a great man; and it's wonderful how he appreciates the Scot, and looks up to his opinion.

> (*But this is a line of conversation in which his Royal Mistress declines to be interested. And she is helped, at that moment,*

by something which really does interest her.)

QUEEN. Brown, how did you come to scratch your leg ?

J. B. 'Twas not me, Ma'am ; 'twas the stable cat did that—just now while Mop was having his walk.

QUEEN. Poor dear Brown ! Did she fly at you ?

J. B. Well, 'twas like this, Ma'am ; first Mop went for her, then she went for him. And I tell ye she'd have scraped his eyes out if I'd left it to a finish.

QUEEN. Ferocious creature ! She must be mad.

J. B. Well, Ma'am, I don't know whether a cat-and-dog fight is a case of what God hath joined together ; but it's the hard thing for man to put asunder ! And that's the scraping I got for it, when I tried.

QUEEN. You must have it cauterised, Brown. I won't have you getting hydrophobia.

J. B. You generally get that from dogs.

QUEEN. Oh, from cats too ; any cat that a mad dog has bitten.

J. B. They do say, Ma'am, that if a mad dog bites you—you have to die barking. So if it's a cat-bite I'm going to die of, you'll hear me mewing the day, maybe.

QUEEN. I don't like cats : I never did. Treacherous, deceitful creatures! Now a dog always looks up to you.

J. B. Yes, Ma'am; they are tasteful, attractive animals; and that, maybe, is the reason. They give you a good conceit of yourself, dogs do. You never have to apologise to a dog. Do him an injury— you've only to say you forgive him, and he's friends again.

> (*Accepting his views with a nodding smile,*
> *she resumes her pen, and spreads paper.*)

QUEEN. Now, Brown, I must get to work again. I have writing to do. See that I'm not disturbed.

J. B. Then when were you wanting to see your visitor, Ma'am? There's his chair waiting.

QUEEN. Ah, yes, to be sure. But I didn't want to worry him too soon. What is the time?

J. B. Nearly twelve, Ma'am.

QUEEN. Oh! then I think I may. Will you go and tell him: the Queen's compliments, and she would like to see him, now?

J. B. I will go and tell him, Ma'am.

QUEEN. And then I shan't want you any more— till this afternoon.

J. B. Then I'll just go across and take lunch at home, Ma'am.

QUEEN. Yes, do! That will be nice for you. And, Brown, mind you have that leg seen to!

25

(Mr. John Brown has started to go, when his step is arrested.)

J. B. His lordship is there in the garden, Ma'am, talking to the Princess.

QUEEN. What, before he has seen *me* ? Go, and take him away from the Princess, and tell him to come here!

J. B. I will, Ma'am.

QUEEN. And you had better take Mop with you. Now, dear Brown, do have your poor leg seen to, at once !

J. B. Indeed, and I will, Ma'am. Come, Mop, man ! Come and tell his lordship he's wanted.

(Exit Mr. John Brown, nicely accompanied by Mop.)

(Left to herself the Queen administers a feminine touch or two to dress and cap and hair ; then with dignified composure she resumes her writing, and continues to write even when the shadow of her favourite minister crosses the entrance, and he stands hat in hand before her, flawlessly arrayed in a gay frock suit suggestive of the period when male attire was still not only a fashion but an art.

Despite, however, the studied correctness of his costume, face and deportment give signs of haggard fatigue ; and when he bows it is the droop of a weary man, slow in the recovery. Just at the fitting moment for full acceptance of his silent salutation, the Royal Lady lays down her pen.)

QUEEN. Oh, how do you do, my dear Lord Beaconsfield! Good morning; and welcome to Balmoral.

LORD B. *(as he kisses the hand extended to him).* That word from your Majesty brings all its charms to life! What a prospect of beauty I see around me!

QUEEN. You arrived early? I hope you are sufficiently rested.

LORD B. Refreshed, Madam; rest will come later.

QUEEN. You have had a long, tiring journey, I fear.

LORD B. It was long, Madam.

QUEEN. I hope that you slept upon the train?

LORD B. I lay upon it, Ma'am. That is all I can say truly.

QUEEN. Oh, I'm sorry!

LORD B. There were compensations, Ma'am. In my vigil I was able to look forward—to that which is now before me. The morning is beautiful! May I be permitted to enquire if your Majesty's health has benefited?

QUEEN. I'm feeling "bonnie," as we say in Scotland. Life out of doors suits me.

27

LORD B. Ah! This tent light is charming! Then my eyes had not deceived me; your Majesty is already more than better. The tempered sunlight, so tender in its reflections, gives—an interior, one may say—of almost floral delicacy; making these canvas walls like the white petals of an enfolding flower.

QUEEN. Are you writing another of your novels, Lord Beaconsfield? That sounds like composition.

LORD B. Believe me, Madam, only an impromptu.

QUEEN. Now, my dear Lord, pray sit down! I had that chair specially brought for you. Generally I sit here quite alone.

LORD B. Such kind forethought, Madam, over-whelms me! Words are inadequate. I accept, gratefully, the repose you offer me.

> (*He sinks into the chair, and sits motionless and mute, in a weariness that is not the less genuine because it provides an effect. But from one seated in the Royal Presence much is expected; and so it is in a tone of sprightly expectancy that his Royal Mistress now prompts him to his task of entertaining her.*)

QUEEN. Well? And how is everything?

LORD B. (*rousing himself with an effort*). Oh! Pardon! Your Majesty would have me speak on politics, and affairs of State ? I was rapt away for the moment.

QUEEN. Do not be in any hurry, dear Prime Minister.

LORD B. Ah! That word from an indulgent Mistress spurs me freshly to my task. But, Madam, there is almost nothing to tell : politics, like the rest of us, have been taking holiday.

QUEEN. I thought that Mr. Gladstone had been speaking.

LORD B. (*with an airy flourish of courtly disdain*), Oh, yes ! He has been—speaking.

QUEEN. In Edinburgh, quite lately.

LORD B. And in more other places than I can count. Speaking—speaking—speaking. But I have to confess, Madam, that I have not read his speeches. They are composed for brains which can find more leisure than yours, Madam—or mine.

QUEEN. I have read some of them.

LORD B. Your Majesty does him great honour— and yourself some inconvenience, I fear. Those speeches, so great a strain to understand, or even to listen to—my hard duty for now some forty years— are a far greater strain to read.

QUEEN. They annoy me intensely. I have no patience with him !

LORD B. Pardon me, Madam ; if you have read

29

one of his speeches, your patience has been extra-ordinary.

QUEEN. Can't you stop it ?

LORD B. Stop ?—stop what, Madam ? Niagara, the Flood ? That which has no beginning, no limit, has also no end : till, by the operation of nature, it runs dry.

QUEEN. But, surely, he should be stopped when he speaks on matters which may, any day, bring us into war !

LORD B. Then he would be stopped. When the British nation goes to war, Madam, it ceases to listen to reason. Then it is only the beating of its own great heart that it hears : to that goes the marching of its armies, with victory as the one goal. Then, Madam, above reason rises instinct. Against that he will be powerless.

QUEEN. You think so ?

LORD B. I am sure, Madam. If we are drawn into war, his opposition becomes futile. If we are not : well, if we are not, it will not be his doing that we escape that—dire necessity.

QUEEN. But you *do* think it necessary, don't you ?

(*To the Sovereign's impetuous eagerness, so creditable to her heart, he replies with the oracular solemnity by which caution can be sublimated.*)

LORD B. I hope it may not be, Madam. We must

all say that—up till the last moment. It is the only thing we *can* say, to testify the pacifity of our intention when challenged by other Powers.

QUEEN (*touching the newspaper*). This morning's news isn't good, I'm afraid. The Russians are getting nearer to Constantinople.

LORD B. They will never enter it, Madam.

QUEEN. No, they mustn't ! We will not allow it.

LORD B. That, precisely, is the policy of your Majesty's Government. Russia knows that we shall not allow it ; she knows that it will never be. Nevertheless, we may have to make a demonstration.

QUEEN. Do you propose to summon Parliament ?

LORD B. Not Parliament ; no, Madam. Your Majesty's Fleet will be sufficient.

(*This lights a spark ; and the royal mind darts into strategy.*)

QUEEN. If I had my way, Lord Beaconsfield, my Fleet would be in the Baltic to-morrow ; and before another week was over, Petersburg would be under bombardment.

LORD B. (*considerately providing this castle in the air with its necessary foundations*). And Cronstadt would have fallen.

QUEEN (*puzzled for a moment at this naming of a place which had not entered her calculations*). Cronstadt ? Why Cronstadt ?

LORD B. Merely preliminary, Madam. When that fortified suburb has crumbled—the rest will be easy.

QUEEN. Yes! And what a good lesson it will teach them! The Crimea wasn't enough for them, I suppose.

LORD B. The Crimea! Ah, what memories—of heroism—that word evokes! " Magnificent, but not war ! "

QUEEN. Oh! There is one thing, Lord Beaconsfield, on which I want your advice.

LORD B. Always at your Majesty's disposal.

QUEEN. I wish to confer upon the Sultan of Turkey my Order of the Garter.

LORD B. Ah! how generous, how generous an instinct! How like you, Madam, to wish it!

QUEEN. What I want to know is, whether, as Prime Minister, you have any objection?

LORD B. " As Prime Minister." How hard that makes it for me to answer! How willingly would I say " None " ! How reluctantly, on the contrary, I have to say, " It had better wait."

QUEEN. Wait? Wait till when? I want to do it *now*.

LORD B. Yes, so do I. But can you risk, Madam, conferring that most illustrious symbol of honour, and chivalry, and power, on a defeated monarch? Your royal prestige, Ma'am, must be considered

32

Great and generous hearts need, more than most, to take prudence into their counsels.

QUEEN. But do you think, Lord Beaconsfield, that the Turks are going to be beaten ?

LORD B. The Turks *are* beaten, Madam. . . . But England will never be beaten. We shall dictate terms—moderating the demands of Russia ; and under your Majesty's protection the throne of the Kaliphat will be safe—once more. That, Madam, is the key to our Eastern policy : a grateful Kaliphat, claiming allegiance from the whole Mahometan world, bound to us by instincts of self-preservation— and we hold henceforth the gorgeous East in fee with redoubled security. His power may be a declining power ; but ours remains. Some day, who knows ? Egypt, possibly even Syria, Arabia, may be our destined reward.

> (*Like a cat over a bowl of cream, England's
> Majesty sits lapping all this up. But,
> when he has done, her commentary is
> shrewd and to the point.*)

QUEEN. The French won't like that !

LORD B. They won't, Madam, they won't. But has it ever been England's policy, Madam, to mind what the French don't like ?

QUEEN (*with relish*). No, it never has been, has

it ?   Ah ! you are the true statesman, Lord Beaconsfield.   Mr. Gladstone never talked to me like that.

LORD B. (*courteously surprised at what does not at
all surprise him*). No ? . . . You must have had
interesting conversations with him, Madam, in the
past.

QUEEN (*very emphatically*).   I have never once had
a conversation with Mr. Gladstone, in all my life,
Lord Beaconsfield. He used to talk to me as if I
were a public meeting—and one that agreed with
him, too !

LORD B.   Was there, then, any applause, Madam ?

QUEEN.   No, indeed !   I was too shy to say what
I thought.   I used to cough sometimes.

LORD B.   Rather like coughing at a balloon, I
fear. I have always admired his flights—regarded
as a mere *tour de force*—so buoyant, so sustained, so
incalculable !   But, as they never touch earth to any
serviceable end, that I could discover—of what use
are they ?   Yet if there is one man who has helped
me in my career—to whom, therefore, I should owe
gratitude—it is he.

QUEEN.   Indeed ?   Now that does surprise me !
Tell me, Lord Beaconsfield, how has he ever helped
you ?

LORD B.   In our party system, Madam, we live
by the mistakes of our opponents. The balance of
34

the popular verdict swings ever this way and that, relegating us either to victory or defeat, to office or to opposition   Many times have I trodden the road to power, or passed from it again, over ruins the origin of which I could recognise either as my own work or that of another ; and most of all has it been over the disappointments, the disaffections, the disgusts, the disillusionments—chiefly among his own party— which my great opponent has left me to profit by. I have gained experience from what he has been morally blind to ; what he has lacked in under- standing of human nature he has left for me to discover. Only to-day I learn that he has been in the habit of addressing—as you, Madam, so wittily phrased it—of addressing, " as though she were a public meeting," that Royal Mistress, whom it has ever been my most difficult task not to address sometimes as the most charming, the most accom- plished, and the most fascinating woman of the epoch which bears her name. (*He pauses, then resumes.*) How strange a fatality directs the fate of each one of us ! How fortunate is he who knows the limits that destiny assigns to him : limits beyond which no word must be uttered.

> (*His oratorical flight, so buoyant and sus-*
> *tained, having come to its calculated end,*
> *he drops deftly to earth, encountering*
> *directly for the first time the flattered*
> *smile with which the Queen has listened*
> *to him.*)

c

Madam, your kind silence reminds me, in the gentlest, the most considerate way possible, that I am not here to relieve the tedium of a life made lonely by a bereavement equal to your own, in conversation however beguiling, or in quest of a sympathy of which, I dare to say, I feel assured. For, in a sense, it is as to a public assembly, or rather as to a great institution, immemorially venerable and august that I have to address myself when, obedient to your summons, I come to be consulted as your Majesty's First Minister of State. If, therefore, your royal mind have any inquiries, any further commands to lay upon me, I am here, Madam, to give effect to them in so far as I can.

> (*This time he has really finished, but with so artful an abbreviation at the point where her interest has been most roused that the Queen would fain have him go on. And so the conversation continues to flow along intimate channels.*)

QUEEN. No, dear Lord Beaconsfield, not to-day! Those official matters can wait. After you have said so much, and said it so beautifully, I would rather still talk with you as a friend. Of friends you and I have not many; those who make up our world, for the most part, we have to keep at a distance. But while I have many near relatives, children and descendants, I remember that you have none. So your case is the harder.

36

LORD B. Ah, no, Madam, indeed! I have my children—descendants who will live after me, I trust—in those policies which, for the welfare of my beloved country, I confide to the care of a Sovereign whom I revere and love. . . . I am not unhappy in my life, Madam ; far less in my fortune ; only, as age creeps on, I find myself so lonely, so solitary, that sometimes I have doubt whether I am really alive, or whether the voice, with which now and then I seek to reassure myself, be not the voice of a dead man.

QUEEN (*almost tearfully*). No, no, my dear Lord Beaconsfield, you mustn't say that !

LORD B. (*gallantly*). I won't say anything, Madam, that you forbid, or that you dislike. You invited me to speak to you as a friend ; so I have done, so I do. I apologise that I have allowed sadness, even for a moment, to trouble the harmony—the sweetness—of our conversation.

QUEEN. Pray, do not apologise ! It has been a very great privilege ; I beg that you will go on ! Tell me—you spoke of bereavement—I wish you would tell me more—about your wife.

> (*The sudden request touches some latent chord ; and it is with genuine emotion that he answers.*)

LORD B. Ah ! My wife ! To her I owed everything.

37

QUEEN. She was devoted to you, wasn't she?

LORD B. I never read the depth of her devotion—till after her death. Then, Madam—this I have told to nobody but yourself—then I found among her papers—addressed "to my dear husband"—a message, written only a few days before her death, with a hand shaken by that nerve-racking and fatal malady which she endured so patiently—begging me to marry again.

(The Queen is now really crying, and finds speech difficult.)

QUEEN. And you, you—? Dear Lord Beaconsfield; did you mean—had you ever meant—— ?

LORD B. I did not then, Madam ; nor have I ever done so since. It is enough if I allow myself—to love.

QUEEN. Oh, yes, yes ; I understand—better than others would. For that has always been my own feeling.

LORD B. In the history of my race, Madam, there has been a great tradition of faithfulness between husbands and wives. For the hardness of our hearts, we are told, Moses permitted us to give a writing of divorcement. But we have seldom acted on it. In my youth I became a Christian ; I married a Christian. But that was no reason for me to desert the nobler traditions of my race—for they are in the blood and in the heart. When my wife died I had

38

no thought to marry again ; and when I came upon that tender wish, still I had no thought for it ; my mind would not change. Circumstances that have happened since have sealed irrevocably my resolution—never to marry again.

QUEEN. Oh, I think that is so wise, so right, so noble of you !

> (*The old Statesman rises, pauses, appears to hesitate, then in a voice charged with emotion says*)

LORD B. Madam, will you permit me to kiss your hand ?

> (*The hand graciously given, and the kiss fervently implanted, he falls back once more to a respectful distance. But the emotional excitement of the interview has told upon him, and it is in a wavering voice of weariness that he now speaks.*)

LORD B. You have been very forbearing with me, Madam, not to indicate that I have outstayed either my welcome or your powers of endurance. Yet so much conversation must necessarily have tired you. May I then crave permission, Madam, to withdraw ? For, to speak truly, I do need some rest.

QUEEN. Yes, my dear friend, go and rest yourself ! But before you go, will you not wait, and take a glass of wine with me ?

39

(He bows, and she rings.)

And there is just one other thing I wish to say before we part.

LORD B.   Speak, Madam, for thy servant heareth.

(The other servant is now also standing to attention, awaiting orders.)

QUEEN.   Bring some wine.

(The Attendant GOES.)

That Order of the Garter which I had intended to confer upon the Sultan—have you, as Prime Minister, any objection if I bestow it nearer home, on one to whom personally—I cannot say more—on yourself, I mean.

(At that pronouncement of the royal favour, the Minister stands, exhausted of energy, in an attitude of drooping humility. The eloquent silence is broken presently by the Queen.)

QUEEN.   Dear Lord Beaconsfield, I want your answer.

LORD B.   Oh, Madam! What adequate answer can these poor lips make to so magnificent an offer? Yet answer I must. We have spoken together briefly to-day of our policies in the Near East. Madam, let me come to you again when I have saved Constantinople, and secured once more upon a firm basis the peace of Europe. Then ask me again whether I have any objection, and I will own—" I have none ! "

> (RE-ENTERS *Attendant. He deposits a tray with decanter and glasses, and retires again.*)

QUEEN. Very well, Lord Beaconsfield. And if you do not remind me, I shall remind you. (*She points to the tray.*) Pray, help yourself !

> (*He takes up the decanter.*)

LORD B. I serve you, Madam ?

QUEEN. Thank you.

> (*He fills the two glasses ; presents hers to the Queen, and takes up his own.*)

LORD B. May I propose for myself—a toast, Madam ?

> (*The Queen sees what is coming, and bows graciously.*)

LORD B. The Queen ! God bless her !

> (*He drains the glass, then breaks it against the pole of the tent, and throws away the stem.*)

An old custom, Madam, observed by loyal defenders of the House of Stewart, so that no lesser health might ever be drunk from the same glass. To my old hand came a sudden access of youthful enthusiasm —an ardour which I could not restrain. Your pardon, Madam !

QUEEN (*very gently*). Go and lie down, Lord Beaconsfield ; you need rest.

LORD B. Adieu, Madam.

QUEEN. Draw your curtains, and sleep well !

> (*For a moment he stands gazing at her with a look of deep emotion ; he tries to speak. Ordinary words seem to fail ; he falters into poetry.*)

" When pain and anguish wring the brow,
A ministering Angel, thou ! "

> (*It has been beautifully said, they both feel. Silent and slow, with head reverentially bowed, he backs from the Presence.*)
> (*The Queen sits and looks after the retreating figure, then at the broken fragments of glass. She takes up the hand-bell and rings. The Attendant* ENTERS.)

QUEEN. Pick up that broken glass.

> (*The Attendant collects it on the hand-tray which he carries.*)

Bring it to me ! . . . Leave it !

> (*The Attendant deposits the tray before her,
> and* GOES. *Gently the Queen handles
> the broken pieces. Then in a voice of
> tearful emotion she speaks.*)

Such devotion !   Most extraordinary !   Oh ! Albert !
Albert !

> (*And in the sixteenth year of her widowhood
> and the fortieth of her reign the Royal
> Lady bends her head over the fragments
> of broken glass, and weeps happy tears.*)

CURTAIN

His Favourite Flower

Dramatis Personæ

THE STATESMAN   THE DOCTOR
THE HOUSEKEEPER   THE PRIMROSES

His Favourite Flower
A Political Myth Explained

*The eminent old Statesman has not been at all well.
He is sitting up in his room, and his doctor has
come to see him for the third time in three days.
This means that the malady is not yet seriously
regarded: once a day is still sufficient. Nevertheless, he is a woeful wreck to look at; and the
doctor looks at him with the greatest respect, and
listens to his querulous plaint patiently. For that
great dome of silence, his brain, repository of so
many state-secrets, is still a redoubtable instrument: its wit and its magician's cunning have not
yet lapsed into the dull inane of senile decay.
Though fallen from power, after a bad beating at
the polls, there is no knowing but that he may
rise again, and hold once more in those tired old
hands, shiny with rheumatic gout, and now
twitching feebly under the discomfort of a super-
imposed malady, the reins of democratic and
imperial power. The dark, cavernous eyes still
wear their look of accumulated wisdom, a touch*

47

also of visionary fire. The sparse locks, dyed to a raven black, set off with their uncanny sheen the clay-like pallor of the face. He sits in a high-backed chair, wrapped in an oriental dressing-gown, his muffled feet resting on a large hot-water bottle ; and the eminent physician, preparatory to taking a seat at his side, bends solicitously over him.

DOCTOR. Well, my dear lord, how are you to-day ? Better ? You look better.

STATESMAN. Yes, I suppose I am better. But my sleep isn't what it ought to be. I have had a dream, Doctor ; and it has upset me.

DOCTOR. A dream ?

STATESMAN. You wonder that I should mention it ? Of course, I—I don't believe in dreams. Yet they indicate, sometimes—do they not ?—certain disorders of the mind.

DOCTOR. Generally of the stomach.

STATESMAN. Ah ! The same thing, Doctor. There's no getting away from that in one's old age ; when one has lived as well as I have.

DOCTOR. That is why I dieted you.

STATESMAN. Oh, I have nothing on my conscience as to that. My housekeeper is a dragon. Her fidelity is of the kind that will even risk dismissal.

DOCTOR. An invaluable person, under the circumstances.

STATESMAN. Yes; a nuisance, but indispensable. No, Doctor. This dream didn't come from the stomach. It seemed rather to emanate from that outer darkness which surrounds man's destiny. So real, so horribly real!

DOCTOR. Better, then, not to brood on it.

STATESMAN. Ah! Could I explain it, then I might get rid of it. In the ancient religion of my race dreams found their interpretation. But have they any?

DOCTOR. Medical science is beginning to say "Yes"; that in sleep the subconscious mind has its reactions.

STATESMAN. Well, I wonder how my "subconscious mind" got hold of primroses.

DOCTOR. Primroses? Did they form a feature in your dream?

STATESMAN. A feature? No. The whole place was alive with them! As the victim of inebriety sees snakes, I saw primroses. They were everywhere: they fawned on me in wreaths and festoons; swarmed over me like parasites; flew at me like flies; till it seemed that the whole world had conspired to suffocate me under a sulphurous canopy of those detestable little atoms. Can you imagine the horror of it, Doctor, to a sane—a hitherto sane mind like mine ?

DOCTOR. Oh ! In a dream any figment may excite aversion.

STATESMAN. This wasn't like a dream. It was rather the threat of some new disease, some brain malady about to descend on me : possibly delirium tremens. I have not been of abstemious habits, Doctor. Suppose—— ?

DOCTOR. Impossible ! Dismiss altogether that supposition from your mind !

STATESMAN. Well, Doctor, I hope—I hope you may be right. For I assure you that the horror I then conceived for those pale botanical specimens in their pestiferous and increscent abundance, exceeded what words can describe. I have felt spiritually devastated ever since, as though some vast calamity were about to fall not only on my own intellect, but on that of my country. Well, you shall hear.

(*He draws his trembling hands wearily over his face, and sits thinking awhile.*)

With all the harsh abruptness of a soul launched into eternity by the jerk of the hangman's rope, so I found myself precipitated into the midst of this dream. I was standing on a pillory, set up in Parliament Square, facing the Abbey. I could see the hands of St. Margaret's clock pointing to half-past eleven; and away to the left the roof of Westminster Hall undergoing restoration. Details, Doctor, which gave a curious reality to a scene otherwise fantastic, unbelievable. There I stood in a pillory, raised up from earth; and a great crowd had gathered to look at me. I can only describe it as a primrose crowd. The disease infected all, but not so badly as it did me. The yellow contagion spread everywhere; from all the streets around, the botanical deluge continued to flow in upon me. I felt a pressure at my back; a man had placed a ladder against it; he mounted and hung a large wreath of primroses about my neck. The sniggering crowd applauded the indignity. Having placed a smaller wreath upon my head, he descended. . . . A mockery of a May Queen, there I stood!

DOCTOR (*laying a soothing hand on him*). A dream, my dear lord, only a dream.

STATESMAN. Doctor, imagine my feelings! My sense of ridicule was keen; but keener my sense of the injustice—not to be allowed to know *why* the whole world was thus making mock of me. For this was in the nature of a public celebration, its malignity was organised and national; a new fifth of November had been sprung upon the calendar. Around me I saw the emblematic watchwords of the great party I had once led to triumph: "Imperium et Libertas," "Peace with Honour," "England shall reign where'er the sun," and other mottoes of a like kind ; and on them also the floral disease had spread itself. The air grew thick and heavy with its sick-room odour. Doctor, I could have vomited.

DOCTOR. Yes, yes ; a touch of biliousness, I don't doubt.

STATESMAN. With a sudden flash of insight— " This," I said to myself, " is my Day of Judgment. Here I stand, judged by my fellow-countrymen, for the failures and shortcomings of my political career. The good intentions with which my path was strewn are now turned to my reproach. But why do they take this particular form ?   Why—why primroses ? "

DOCTOR. " The primrose way " possibly ?

STATESMAN. Ah ! That occurred to me. But has it, indeed, been a primrose way that I have trodden so long and so painfully ?   I think not.   I cannot so accuse myself. But suppose the Day of Judgment which Fate reserves for us were fundamentally this : the appraisement of one's life and character—not by the all-seeing Eye of Heaven (before which I would bow), but by the vindictively unjust verdict of the people one has tried to serve—the judgment not of God, but of public opinion. That is a judgment of which all who strive for power must admit the relevancy !

DOCTOR. You distress yourself unnecessarily, dear lord. Your reputation is safe from detraction now.

STATESMAN. With urgency I set my mind to meet the charge. If I could understand the meaning of that yellow visitation, then I should no longer have to fear that I was going mad!

> (*At this point the door is discreetly opened, and the Housekeeper, mild, benign, but inflexible,* ENTERS, *carrying a cup and toast-rack upon a tray.*)

HOUSEKEEPER. I beg pardon, my lord; but I think your lordship ought to have your beef-tea now.

STATESMAN. Yes, yes, Mrs. Manson; come in.

DOCTOR. You are right, Mrs. Manson; he ought.

HOUSEKEEPER (*placing the tray on a small stand*). Where will you have it, my lord?

STATESMAN. In my inside, Mrs. Manson—presently —he, he!

DOCTOR. Now, let me take your pulse. . . . Yes, yes. Pretty good, you know.

> (*Mrs. Manson stands respectfully at attention with interrogation in her eye.*)

STATESMAN. Yes, you may bring me my cap now. (*Then to the Doctor*). I generally sleep after this.

> (*Mrs. Manson brings a large tasselled fez of brilliant colour, and adjusts it to his head while he drinks. She then goes to the*

53

door, takes a hot-water bottle from the hands of an unseen servant and effects the necessary changes. All this is done so unobtrusively that the Statesman resumes his theme without regarding her. When she has done she goes.)

Ah! Where was I?

DOCTOR. If you " could understand," you said.

STATESMAN. Ah, yes; understand. Again a strange faculty of divination came upon me. I stood upon the international plane, amid a congress of Powers, and let my eye travel once more over the Alliances of Europe. I looked, Doctor, and truly I saw, then, surprising shifts and changes in the political and diplomatic fabric which I had helped to frame. Time, and kingdoms had passed. I saw, at home and abroad, the rise of new parties into power, strange coalitions, defections, alliances ; old balances destroyed, new balances set up in their place. I saw frontiers annulled, treaties violated, world-problems tumbling like clowns, standing on their heads and crying, " Here we are again ! " Power—after all, had solved nothing !

My eye travelled over that problem of the Near East, which, for some generations at least, we thought to have settled, to Vienna, Petersburg, Constantinople —and away farther East to Teheran and—that other place whose name I have forgotten. And, as I looked, a Recording Angel came, and cried to me in a voice strangely familiar, the voice of one of my most detested colleagues—trusted, I mean—"You have put your money on the wrong horse!"

And I had, Doctor; if what I saw then was true— I had! Yes, if ever man blundered and fooled his countrymen into a false and fatal position—I was that man! It wasn't a question of right or wrong. In politics that doesn't really matter; you decide on a course, and you invent moral reasons for it afterwards. No, what I had done was much worse than any mere wrongdoing. All my political foresight and achievements were a gamble that had gone wrong; and for that my Day of Judgment had come, and I stood in the pillory, a peepshow for mockery. But why for their instrument of torture did they choose primroses? Oh, I can invent a reason! It was Moses Primrose, cheated of his horse with a gross of green spectacles cased in shagreen. But that was not the reason. For then came new insight, and a fresh humiliation. As I looked more intently I saw that I was *not* being mocked; I was being worshipped, adulated, flattered; I had become a god—for party purposes perhaps—and this was my day, given in my honour for national celebration. And I saw, by the insight given me, that they were praising me *for having put their money on the wrong horse!* Year by year the celebration had gone on, until they had so got into the habit that they could not leave off! All my achievements, all my policies, all my statecraft were in the dust; but the worship of me had become

55

a national habit—so foolish and meaningless, that nothing, nothing but some vast calamity—some great social upheaval, was ever going to stop it.

DOCTOR. My dear lord, it is I who must stop it now. You mustn't go on.

STATESMAN. I have done, Doctor. There I have given you the essentials of my dream ; material depressing enough for the mind of an old man, enfeebled by indisposition, at the end of a long day's work. But I tell you, Doctor, that nothing therein which stands explainable fills me with such repulsion and aversion as that one thing which I cannot explain —why, why primroses ?

DOCTOR. A remarkable dream, my lord ; rendered more vivid—or, as you say, " real "—by your present disturbed state of health. As to that part of it which you find so inexplicable, I can at least point toward where the explanation lies. It reduces itself to this : primroses had become associated for you— in a way which you have forgotten—with something you wished to avoid. And so they became the image, or symbol, of your aversion ; and as such found a place in your dream.

(*So saying the doctor rises and moves toward the window, where his attention suddenly becomes riveted.*)

STATESMAN. Perhaps, Doctor, perhaps, as you say, there is some such explanation. But I don't feel like that.

DOCTOR. Why, here are primroses! This may be the clue? Where do they come from?

STATESMAN. Ah, those! Indeed, I had forgotten them. At least; no, I could not have done that.

DOCTOR. There is a written card with them, I see.

STATESMAN. Her Gracious Majesty did me the great honour, hearing that I was ill, to send and inquire. Of course, since my removal from office, the opportunity of presenting my personal homage has not been what it used to be. That, I suppose, is as well.

DOCTOR. And these are from her Majesty?

STATESMAN. They came yesterday, brought by a special messenger, with a note written by her own hand, saying that she had picked them herself. To so great a condescension I made with all endeavour what return I could. I wrote—a difficult thing for me to do, Doctor, just now—presented my humble duty, my thanks; and said they were my favourite flower.

DOCTOR. And were they?

STATESMAN. Of course, Doctor, under those circumstances any flower would have been. It just happened to be that.

DOCTOR. Well, my lord, there, then, the matter is explained. You *had* primroses upon your mind.

The difficulty, the pain even, of writing with your crippled hand, became associated with them. You would have much rather not had to write; and the disinclination, in an exaggerated form, got into your dream. Now that, I hope, mitigates for you the annoyance—the distress of mind.

STATESMAN. Yes, yes. It does, as you say, make it more understandable. Bring them to me, Doctor; let me look my enemy in the face.

> (*The Doctor carries the bowl across and sets it beside him. Very feebly he reaches out a hand and takes some.*)

My favourite flower. He—he! My favourite flower.

> (*Lassitude overtakes him—his head nods and droops as he speaks.*)

A primrose by the river's brim
A yellow primrose was to him,
    And it was nothing more.

Who was it wrote that?—Byron or Dr. Watts? My memory isn't what it used to be. No matter. It all goes into the account.

My favourite flower!

" For I'm to be Queen of the May, mother, I'm to be Queen of the May ! "

> (*The Doctor takes up his hat, and tiptoes to the door.*)

Tell me, where is fancy bred,
  Or in the heart or in the head ?
How begot, how nourished ?

(He breaks, and lets the petals fall one by one)
(The Doctor goes out.)

Let us all ring fancy's knell ;
  I'll begin it—Ding-dong bell,
    Ding-dong, bell.

(He goes to sleep.)

CURTAIN

The Comforter

Dramatis Personæ

W. E. GLADSTONE   MR. ARMITSTEAD

MRS. GLADSTONE   MR. JOHN MORLEY

A FOOTMAN

The Comforter

A Political Finale

*The Scene is a sitting-room in Downing Street. The
date March, 1894. The time 10.30 p.m.*

*Mrs. Gladstone sits before the fire, on a sofa com-
fortable for two, finishing off a piece of knitting.
Apparently she has just rung the bell, on the
arrival from the dining-room of her husband and
his two guests, for presently the door opens and
the footman presents himself for orders. Mr. Gladstone takes down from the bookshelf a backgammon
board, which he opens upon a small table somewhat
distant from the fireplace.*

GLADSTONE. Well, Armitstead, draughts, or backgammon ?

ARMITSTEAD.   It was backgammon you promised
me.

GLADSTONE.   A rubber ?

ARMITSTEAD.   I shall be delighted.

> (*They seat themselves, and begin to set the
> board. Mr. Morley stands detached
> looking on, grave, not quite at ease.*)

63

MRS. G. (*to the footman*). James, bring up the wine and some biscuits.

JAMES. Whisky, madam ?

MRS. G. No, no ; biscuits. Soft biscuits for the other gentlemen, and some hard ones for the master.

JAMES. Yes, madam.

> (*He goes, and in a few minutes returns, sets wine and biscuits on the side-table, and retires.*)

MORLEY (*to* GLADSTONE). Now ?

GLADSTONE. If you will be so good, my dear Morley, I shall be much obliged.

> (*Slowly and thoughtfully Mr. Morley goes over to fireplace, where he stands looking at Mrs. Gladstone, who is now beginning to " cast-off " a completed piece of knitting. The rattle of the dice is heard.*)

GLADSTONE. You play.

> (*Thereafter, as the game proceeds, the dice are heard constantly.*)

MORLEY. Well, dear lady ?

MRS. G. Well, Mr. Morley ? So Mr. Gladstone is at his game, and has sent you to talk to me.

MORLEY. Precisely. You have guessed right.

MRS. G.   He always thinks of me.

MORLEY.   Yes.

MRS. G.   Won't you sit down, Mr. Morley ?

MORLEY.   By you ?   With pleasure.

MRS. G.   And how is the world using you ?

MORLEY.   Like Balaam's ass.   The angel of the Lord stands before me with a drawn sword, and my knees quail under me.

MRS. G.   I thought you didn't believe in angels, Mr. Morley.

MORLEY.   In the scriptural sense, no.   In the political, they are rare ; but one meets them—sometimes.

MRS. G.   And then they frighten you ?

MORLEY.   They make a coward of me.   I want to temporise—put off the inevitable.   But it's no good. Angels have to be faced.   That's the demand they make on us.

MRS. G.   You have something on your mind.

MORLEY.   Yes.   But we'll not talk about it—yet.

MRS. G.   I have something on mine.

MORLEY.   Anything serious ?

MRS. G.   It concerns you, Mr. Morley.   Would you

65

very much mind accepting a gift not originally intended for you ?

MORLEY. I have accepted office on those terms before now.

MRS. G. Ah ! Mr. Gladstone has always so trusted you.

MORLEY. Yes.

MRS. G. More than he has most people.

MORLEY. I have been finding that out. It has become a habit, I'm afraid. I can't cure him.

MRS. G. What I had on my mind, Mr. Morley, was this : I have knitted this comforter for you ; at least, it's for you if you would like it.

MORLEY. Angel !

MRS. G. Does that mean that you don't want it ?

MORLEY. Oh, no ! It will be very good discipline for me ; made by you, I shall have to wear it.

MRS. G. But you know, it's a very remarkable thing that I *can* offer it you. Ever since we married I have been knitting comforters for Mr. Gladstone, which he has always either been losing or giving away. This is the first time I have been able to get ahead of him. He still has two. Isn't that a triumph ?

MORLEY. It is, indeed.

66

MRS. G. He's more careful now, and doesn't lose them. He begins to feel, I suppose, that he's getting old—and needs them.

MORLEY. You surprise me! Why, he is not yet ninety!

MRS. G. Do you know, he still sleeps like a child! Sometimes I lie awake to watch him. It's wonderful.

MORLEY. It's habit, madam; that, and force of will.

MRS. G. And really it is only then I can feel that he quite belongs to me. All the rest of the time it's a struggle.

MORLEY. In which you have won.

MRS. G. Have I?

MORLEY. Every time.

MRS. G. (*wistfully*). Do I, Mr. Morley?

MORLEY. It is you, more than anything, who have kept him young.

MRS. G. Oh, no! I'm the ageing influence.

MORLEY. I don't believe it.

MRS. G. Yes; I stand for caution, prudence. He's like a great boy. . . . You don't think so; you see the other side of his character. But here have I been, sixty years, trying to make him take advice!

E

MORLEY. And sometimes succeeding. Gods, and their makers ! What a strange world !

MRS. G. Spending one's life feeding a god on beef-tea, that's been my work. (*The dear lady sighs.*)

MORLEY. And making comforters for him.

MRS. G. It's terrible when he won't take it !

MORLEY. The beef-tea ?

MRS. G. No, the advice. For I'm generally right, you know.

MORLEY. I can well believe it. Strange to think how the welfare and destiny of the nation have sometimes lain here—in this gentle hand.

MRS. G. We do jump in the dark so, don't we ? Who can say what is really best for anyone ?

MORLEY. And prescribing for a god is more difficult.

MRS. G. Much more.

MORLEY. So when he comes to ask a mere mortal for advice—well, now you must judge how difficult it has been for *me* !

MRS. G. Have you been giving him advice ?

MORLEY. In a way ; yes.

MRS. G. And has he taken it ?

MORLEY. A few days ago he told me of a resolution

68

he had come to. I could not disapprove. But now I wonder how it is going to strike *you* ?

MRS. G. Has anything special happened ? He has not told me.

MORLEY (*gravely*). To-morrow, or the day after, he will be going down to Windsor.

MRS. G. Oh, I'm sorry ! That always depresses him. He and the Queen don't get on very well together.

MORLEY. They will get on well enough this time, I imagine.

MRS. G. (*a little bit alarmed*). Does that mean— any change of policy ?

MORLEY. Of policy—I hope not. Of person—yes.

MRS. G. Is anyone leaving the Cabinet ?

MORLEY. We may all be leaving it, very soon. He asked me to tell you ; he had promised Armitstead a game. Look how he is enjoying it !

MRS. G. (*shrewdly*). Ah ! then I expect he is winning.

MORLEY. Oh ? I should not have called him a bad loser.

MRS. G. No ; but he likes winning better—the excitement of it.

MORLEY. That is only human. Yes, he has been a great winner—sometimes.

MRS. G. When has he ever lost—except just for the time ? He always knows that.

MORLEY. Ah, yes ! To quote your own sprightly phrase, we—he and the party with him—are always " popping up again."

MRS. G. When did I say that ?

MORLEY. Seven years ago, when we began to win bye-elections on the Irish question. The bye-elections are not going so well for us just now.

MRS. G. But the General Election will.

MORLEY. Perhaps one will—in another seven years or so.

MRS. G. But isn't there to be one this year ?

MORLEY (*gravely*). The Cabinet has decided against it.

MRS. G. But Mr. Morley ! Now the Lords have thrown out the Irish Bill there must be an election.

MORLEY. That was Mr. Gladstone's view.

MRS. G. Wasn't it yours, too ?

MORLEY. Yes ; but we couldn't—we couldn't carry the others.

MRS. G. Then you mean Mr. Gladstone is going to form a new Cabinet ?

MORLEY. No. A new Cabinet is going to be formed, but he will not be in it. That is his resolution. I was to tell you.

> (*At this news of the downfall of her hopes the gentle face becomes piteously woeful ; full of wonder also.*)

MRS. G. He asked you—to tell me that !

MORLEY. Yes.

MRS. G. Oh ! Then he really means it ! Had he been in any doubt he would have consulted me.

> (*Tears have now come to sustain the dear lady in her sense of desolation. Mr. Morley, with quiet philosophy, does his best to give comfort.*)

MORLEY. It was the only thing to do. Ireland kept him in politics ; if that goes, he goes with it.

MRS. G. But Ireland—doesn't go.

MORLEY. As the cause for a General Election it goes, I'm afraid.

MRS. G. But that isn't honest, Mr. Morley !

MORLEY. I agree.

MRS. G. And it won't do any good—not in the end.

MORLEY. To that also, I agree. Ireland remains ; and the problem will get worse.

MRS. G.   But, indeed, you are wrong, Mr. Morley! It was not Ireland that kept my husband in politics; it was Mr. Chamberlain.

MORLEY.   That is a view which, I confess, had not occurred to me.   Chamberlain?

MRS. G.   No one could have kept Mr. Chamberlain from leading the Liberal party, except Mr. Gladstone.   And now he never will!

MORLEY.   That, certainly, is a triumph, of a kind. You think that influenced him?   Chamberlain was a friend of mine once—is still, in a way.   (*He pauses, then adds ruefully*) Politics are a cruel game!

> (*He sighs and sits depressed.   But mention of her husband's great antagonist has made the old lady brisk again.*)

MRS. G.   Do you know, Mr. Morley, that if Mr. Gladstone had not made me pray for that man every night of my life, I should positively have hated him.

MORLEY (*with a touch of mischief*).   You do that? —still?   Tell me—(I am curious)—do you pray for him as plain " Joe Chamberlain," or do you put in the " Mister "?

MRS. G.   I never mention his name at all; I leave that to Providence—to be understood.

MORLEY.   Well, it *has* been understood, and

72

answered—abundantly; Chamberlain's star is in the ascendant again. It's strange; he and Mr. Gladstone never really got on together.

MRS. G. I don't think he ever really tried—much.

MORLEY. Didn't he? Oh, you don't mean Mr. Gladstone?

MRS. G. And then, you see, the Queen never liked him. That has counted for a good deal.

MORLEY. It has—curiously.

MRS. G. Now why should it, Mr. Morley? She ought not to have such power—any more than I.

MORLEY. How can it be kept from either of you? During the last decade this country has been living on two rival catchwords, which in the field of politics have meant much—the "Widow at Windsor," and the "Grand Old Man." And these two makers of history are mentally and temperamentally incompatible. That has been the tragedy. This is *her* day, dear lady; but it won't always be so.

MRS. G. Mr. Morley, who is going to be—who will take Mr. Gladstone's place?

MORLEY. Difficult to say: the Queen may make her own choice. Spencer, perhaps; though I rather doubt it; probably Harcourt.

MRS. G. Shall you serve under him?

MORLEY. I haven't decided.

MRS. G. You won't.

MORLEY. Possibly not. We are at the end of a dispensation. Whether I belong to the new one, I don't yet know.

MRS. G. The Queen will be pleased, at any rate.

MORLEY. Delighted.

MRS. G. Will she offer him a peerage, do you think?

MORLEY. Oh, of course.

MRS. G. Yes. And she knows he won't accept it. So that gives her the advantage of seeming—magnanimous!

MORLEY. Dear lady, you say rather terrible things—sometimes! You pray for the Queen, too, I suppose; or don't you?

MRS. G. Oh yes; but that's different. I don't feel with her that it's personal. She was always against him. It was her bringing up; she couldn't help being.

MORLEY. So was Chamberlain; so was Harcourt; so was everybody. He is the loneliest man, in a great position, that I have ever known.

MRS. G. Till he met you, Mr. Morley.

MORLEY. I was only speaking of politics. Sixty years ago he met *you*.

MRS. G. Nearly sixty-three.

MORLEY. Three to the good; all the better!

MRS. G. (*having finished off the comforter*). There ! that is finished now !

MORLEY. A thousand thanks ; so it is to be mine, is it ?

MRS. G. I wanted to say, Mr. Morley, how good I think you have always been to me.

MORLEY. I, dear lady ? I ?

MRS. G. I must so often have been in the way without knowing it. You see, you and I think differently. We belong to different schools.

MORLEY. If you go on, I shall have to say " angel," again. That is all I *can* say.

MRS. G. (*tremulously*). Oh, Mr. Morley, you will tell me ! Is this the end ? Has he—has he, after all, been a failure ?

MORLEY. My dear lady, he has been an epoch.

MRS. G. Aren't epochs failures, sometimes ?

MORLEY. Even so, they count ; we have to reckon with them. No, he is no failure ; though it may seem like it just now. Don't pay too much attention to what the papers will say. He doesn't, though he reads them. Look at him now !—does that look like failure ?

> (*He points to the exuberantly energetic figure
> intensely absorbed in its game.*)

MRS. G. He is putting it on to-night a little, for

me, Mr. Morley. He knows I am watching him. Tell me how he seemed when he first spoke to you. Was he feeling it—much?

MORLEY. Oh, deeply, of course! He believes that on a direct appeal we could win the election.

MRS. G. And you?

MORLEY. I don't. But all the same I hold it the right thing to do. Great causes must face and number their defeats. That is how they come to victory.

MRS. G. And now that will be in other hands, not his. Suppose he should not live to see it. Oh, Mr. Morley, Mr. Morley, how am I going to bear it!

MORLEY. Dear lady, I don't usually praise the great altitudes. May I speak in his praise, just for once, to-night? As a rather faithless man myself—not believing or expecting too much of human nature—I see him now, looking back, more than anything else as a man of faith.

MRS. G. Ah, yes. To him religion has always meant everything.

MORLEY. Faith in himself, I meant.

MRS. G. Of course; he had to have that, too.

MORLEY. And I believe in him still, more now than ever. They can remove him; they cannot remove Ireland. He may have made mistakes and misjudged characters; he may not have solved the

76

immediate problem either wisely or well. But **this** he has done, to our honour and to his own : he has given us the cause of liberty as a sacred trust. If we break faith with that, we ourselves shall be broken—and we shall deserve it.

MRS. G. You think that—possible ?

MORLEY. I would rather not think anything just now. The game is over ; I must be going. Good night, dear friend ; and if you sleep only as well as you deserve, I could wish you no better repose. Good-bye.

> (*He moves toward the table from which the players are now rising.*)

GLADSTONE. That is a game, my dear Armitstead, which came to this country nearly eight hundred years ago from the Crusades. Previously it had been in vogue among the nomadic tribes of the Arabian desert for more than a thousand years. Its very name, "backgammon," so English in sound, is but a corruption from the two Arabic words *bacca*, and *gamma* (my pronunciation of which stands subject to correction), meaning—if I remember rightly— "the board game." There, away East, lies its origin ; its first recorded appearance in Europe was at the Sicilian Court of the Emperor Frederick II ; and when the excommunication of Rome fell on him in the year 1283, the game was placed under an interdict, which, during the next four hundred years, was secretly but sedulously disregarded within those impregnably fortified places of learning and piety, to which so much of our Western civilisation is due, the abbeys and other scholastic foundations of the Benedictine order. The book-form, in which the board still conceals itself, stands as a memorial of its secretive preservation upon the shelves of the monastic libraries. I keep my own, with a certain touch of ritualistic observance, between this seventeenth century edition of the works of Roger Bacon and this more modern one, in Latin, of the writings of Thomas Aquinas; both of whom may not improbably have been practitioners of the game.

ARMITSTEAD. Very interesting, very interesting.

(*During this recitation Mr. Gladstone has neatly packed away the draughts and the dice, shutting them into their case finally and restoring it to its place upon the bookshelf.*)

GLADSTONE. My dear, I have won the rubber.

MRS. G. Have you, my dear? I'm very glad, if Mr. Armitstead does not mind.

ARMITSTEAD. To be beaten by Mr. Gladstone, ma'am, is a liberal education in itself.

MORLEY (*to his host*). I must say good-night, now, sir.

GLADSTONE. What, my dear Morley, must you be going?

78

MORLEY.   For one of my habits it is almost late—eleven.

ARMITSTEAD.   In that case I must be going, too. Can I drop you anywhere, Morley?

MORLEY.   Any point, not out of your way, in the direction of my own door, I shall be obliged.

ARMITSTEAD.   With pleasure.   I will come at once. And so—good-night, Mrs. Gladstone. Mr. Prime Minister, good-night.

GLADSTONE.   Good-night, Armitstead.

MORLEY (*aside to Mr. Gladstone*).   I have done what you asked of me, sir.

GLADSTONE.   I thank you.   Good-night.

> (*The two guests have gone ; and husband and wife are left alone. He approaches, and stands near.*)

So Morley has told you, my dear?

MRS. G.   That you are going down to Windsor to-morrow?   Yes, William.   You will want your best frock-suit, I suppose?

GLADSTONE.   My best and my blackest would be seemly under the circumstances, my love.   This treble-dated crow will keep the obsequies as strict as Court etiquette requires, or as his wardrobe may allow.   I have a best suit, I suppose?

MRS. G.   Yes, William.   I keep it put away for you.

GLADSTONE (*after a meditative pause begins to recite*).

> " Come, thou who art the wine and wit
>   Of all I've writ :
>   The grace, the glory, and the best
>   Piece of the rest,
>   Thou art, of what I did intend,
>   The all and end ;
>   And what was made, was made to meet
>   Thee, thee, my sheet ! "

Herrick, to his shroud, my dear ! A poet who has the rare gift of being both light and spiritual in the same breath. Read Herrick at his gravest, when you need cheering ; you will always find him helpful.

MRS. G.   Then—will you read him to me to-night, William ?

GLADSTONE.   Why, certainly, my love, if you wish.

(*He stoops and kisses her.*)

MRS. G. (*speaking very gently*).   I was waiting for that.

GLADSTONE.   And I was waiting—for what you have to say.

MRS. G.   I can say nothing.

GLADSTONE.   Why, nothing ?

MRS. G.   Because I can't be sure of you, my dear. You've done this before.

GLADSTONE.   This time it has been done for me.

My own say in the matter has been merely to acquiesce.

MRS. G. Ah! so you say! And others—others may say it for you; but——

GLADSTONE. Anno Domini says it, my dear.

MRS. G. Anno Domini has been saying it for the last twenty years. Much heed you paid to Anno Domini.

GLADSTONE. You never lent it the weight of your counsels, my own love—till now.

MRS. G. I know, William, when talking is useless.

GLADSTONE. Ah! I wonder—if I do.

MRS. G. No; that's why I complain. Twenty years ago you said you were going to retire from politics and take up theology again—that you were old, and had come to an end. Why, you were only just beginning! And it will always be the same; any day something may happen—more Bulgarian atrocities, or a proposal for Welsh disestablishment. Then you'll break out again!

GLADSTONE. But I am in favour of Welsh disestablishment, my dear—when it comes.

MRS. G. Are you? Oh, yes; I forgot. You are in favour of so many things you didn't used to be. Well, then, it will be something else. You will always find an excuse; I shall never feel safe about you.

GLADSTONE (*in moved tone*). And if you could feel safe about me—what then ?

MRS. G. Oh, my dear, my dear, if I could ! Always I've seen you neglecting yourself—always putting aside your real interests—the things that you most inwardly cared about, the things which you always meant to do when you " had time." And here I have had to sit and wait for the time that never came. Isn't that true ?

GLADSTONE. There is an element of truth in it, my dear.

MRS. G. Well, twenty years have gone like that, and you've " had no time." Oh, if you could only go back to the things you meant to do, twenty years ago—and take them up, just where you left off— why, I should see you looking—almost young again. For you've been looking tired lately, my dear.

GLADSTONE. Tired ? Yes : I hoped not to have shown it. But three weeks ago I had to own to myself that I was beginning to feel tired. I went to Crichton Browne (I didn't tell you, my love) ; he said there was nothing the matter with me—except old age.

MRS. G. You should have come to me, my dear · I could have told you the only thing to do.

GLADSTONE. Is it too late to tell me now ?

MRS. G. Yes ; because now you've done it,

without my advice, William. Think of that! For the first time!

GLADSTONE (*gravely surprised*). So you have been wishing it, have you?

> (*And the devoted wife, setting her face, and steadying her voice, struggles on to give him what comfort she may, in the denial of her most cherished hopes.*)

MRS. G. I've been waiting, waiting, waiting for it to come. But it was the one thing I couldn't say, till you—till you thought of it yourself!

GLADSTONE. Did I do so? Or did others think of it for me? I'm not sure; I'm not sure. My judgment of the situation differed from theirs. I couldn't carry them with me. In my own Cabinet I was a defeated man. Only Morley stood by me then.

> (*Deep in the contemplation of his last political defeat, he is not looking at her face; and that is as well. Her voice summons him almost cheerfully from his reverie.*)

MRS. G. William dear, can you come shopping with me to-morrow? Oh, no, to-morrow you are going to Windsor. The day after, then.

GLADSTONE. What is that for, my dear?

MRS. G. We have to get something for Dorothy's

F

birthday, before we go home. You mustn't forget things like that, you know. Dorothy is important.

GLADSTONE. Not merely important, my love; she is a portent—of much that we shall never know. Dorothy will live to see the coming of the new age.

MRS. G. The new age? Well, so long as you let it alone, my dear, it may be as new as it likes; I shan't mind.

GLADSTONE. We will leave Dorothy to manage it her own way.

MRS. G. Then you will shop with me—not to-morrow—Thursday?

GLADSTONE. Piccadilly, or Oxford Street?

MRS. G. I thought Gamage's.

GLADSTONE. Holborn? That sounds adventurous. Yes, my love, I will shop with you on Thursday—if all goes well at Windsor to-morrow—with all the contentment in the world. (*They kiss.*) Now go to bed; and presently I will come and read Herrick to you.

> (*She gets up and goes toward the door, when her attention is suddenly arrested by the carpet.*)

MRS. G. William! Do you see how this carpet is wearing out? We shall have to get a new one.

GLADSTONE. It won't be necessary now. Those

84

at Hawarden, if I remember rightly, are sufficiently new to last out our time.

MRS. G. I wish I could think so, my dear. They would if you didn't give them such hard wear, walking about on them. The way you wear things out has been my domestic tragedy all along !

GLADSTONE (*standing with folded hands before her*). My love, I have just remembered ; I have a confession to make.

MRS. G. What, another ? Oh, William !

GLADSTONE. I cannot find either of my comforters. I'm afraid I have lost them. I had both this morning, and now both are gone.

MRS. G. Why, you are worse than ever, my dear ! Both in one day ! You have not done that for twenty years.

GLADSTONE. I am sorry. I won't do it again.

MRS. G. Ah ! so you say ! Poor Mr. Morley will have to wait now. I had promised him this. There !

> (*Making him sit down, she puts the comforter round his neck, and gives him a parting kiss.*)

And now I'm going.

GLADSTONE. Go, my love ! I will come presently.

> (*But he has not quite got rid of her. Her hands are now reaching down to the back of the sofa behind him.*)

What are you looking for ?

MRS. G. My knitting-needles. You are sitting on them. Now mind, you are not to sit up!

GLADSTONE. I won't sit up long.

> (*Quietly and serenely she goes to the door, looks back for a moment, then glides through it, leaving behind a much-deceived husband, who will not hear the sound of her solitary weeping, or see any signs of it on her face when presently he comes to read Herrick at her bedside.*)

> (*For a while he sits silent, peacefully encompassed in the thoughts with which she has provided him; then very slowly he speaks.*)

GLADSTONE. Well, if it pleases her—I suppose it must be right!

CURTAIN

Possession

Dramatis Personæ

JULIA ROBINSON ⎫	
LAURA JAMES . ⎬ . *Sisters*	
MARTHA ROBINSON ⎭	
SUSAN ROBINSON .	. *Their Mother*
THOMAS ROBINSON .	. *Their Father*
WILLIAM JAMES .	. *Husband to Laura James*
HANNAH . . .	. *The family servant*

Part Two
The Everlasting Habitations

"ALL HOPE ABANDON YE WHO ENTER HERE."

"*Make to yourselves friends of the mammon of unrighteousness; that, when ye fail, they may receive you into everlasting habitations.*"

Possession

A Peep-Show in Paradise

SCENE.—*The Everlasting Habitations*

It is evening (or so it seems), and to the comfortably furnished Victorian drawing-room a middle-aged maid-servant in cap and apron brings a lamp, and proceeds to draw blinds and close curtains. To do this she passes the fire-place, where before a pleasantly bright hearth sits, comfortably sedate, an elderly lady whose countenance and attitude suggest the very acme of genteel repose. She is a handsome woman, very conscious of herself, but carrying the burden of her importance with an ease which, in her own mind, leaves nothing to be desired. The once-striking outline of her features has been rounded by good feeding to a softness which is merely physical; and her voice, when she speaks, has a calculated gentleness very caressing to her own ear, and a little irritating to others who are not of an inferior class. Menials like it, however. The room, though over-upholstered, and not furnished with any more individual taste than that which gave its generic stamp to the great Victorian period, is the happy possessor of some good things.

89

Upon the mantel-shelf, backed by a large mirror, stands old china in alternation with alabaster jars, under domed shades, and tall vases encompassed by pendant ringlets of glass-lustre. Rose-wood, walnut, and mahogany make a well-wooded interior; and in the dates thus indicated there is a touch of Georgian. But, over and above these mellowing features of a respectable ancestry, the annunciating Angel of the Great Exhibition of 1851 has spread a brooding wing. And while the older articles are treasured on account of family association, the younger and newer stand erected in places of honour by reason of an intrinsic beauty never previously attained to. Through this chamber the dashing crinoline has wheeled the too vast orb of its fate, and left fifty years after (if we may measure the times of Heaven by the ticks of an earthly chronometer) a mark which nothing is likely to erase. Upon the small table, where Hannah the servant deposits the lamp, lies a piece of crochet-work. The fair hands that have been employed on it are folded on a lap of corded silk representing the fashions of the nineties, and the grey-haired beauty (that once was) sits contemplative, wearing a cap of creamish lace, tastefully arranged, not unaware that in the entering lamp-light, and under the fire's soft glow of approval, she presents to her domestic's eye an improving picture of gentility. It is to Miss Julia Robinson's credit—and she herself places it there emphatically—that she always treats

*servants humanly, though at a distance. And
when she now speaks she confers her slight remark
just a little as though it were a favour.*

JULIA. How the days are drawing out, Hannah.

HANNAH. Yes, Ma'am; nicely, aren't they?

> (*For Hannah, being old-established, may say
> a thing or two not in the strict order. In
> fact, it may be said that, up to a well-
> understood point, character is encouraged
> in her, and is allowed to peep through in
> her remarks.*)

JULIA. What time is it?

HANNAH (*looking with better eyes than her mistress
at the large ormolu clock which records eternally the time
of the great Exhibition*). Almost a quarter to six,
Ma'am.

JULIA. So late? She ought to have been here
long ago.

HANNAH. Who, Ma'am, did you say, Ma'am?

JULIA. My sister, Mrs. James. You remember?

HANNAH. What, Miss Martha, Ma'am? Well!

JULIA. No, it's Miss Laura this time: you didn't
know she had married, I suppose?

HANNAH (*with a world of meaning, well under control*).
No, Ma'am. (*A pause.*) I made up the bed in the
red room; was that right, Ma'am?

JULIA (*archly surprised*). What? Then you knew

someone was coming? Why did you pretend, Hannah?

HANNAH. Well, Ma'am, you see, you hadn't *told* me before.

JULIA. I couldn't. One cannot always be sure. (*This mysteriously.*) But something tells me now that she is to be with us. I have been expecting her over four days.

HANNAH (*picking her phrases a little, as though on doubtful ground*). It must be a long way, Ma'am. Did she make a comfortable start, Ma'am?

JULIA. Very quietly, I'm told. No pain.

HANNAH. I wonder what she'll be able to eat now, Ma'am. She was always very particular.

JULIA. I daresay you will be told soon enough. (*Thus in veiled words she conveys that Hannah knows something of Mrs. James's character.*)

HANNAH (*resignedly*). Yes, M'm.

JULIA. I don't think I'll wait any longer. If you'll bring in tea now. Make enough for two, in case: pour it off into another pot, and have it under the tea-cosy.

HANNAH. Yes, Ma'am.

> (*Left alone, the dear lady enjoys the sense of herself and the small world of her own thoughts in solitude. Then she sighs indulgently.*)

JULIA. Yes, I suppose I would rather it had been Martha. Poor Laura! (*She puts out her hand for her crochet, when it is arrested by the sound of a knock, rather rapacious in character.*) Ah, that's Laura all over!

> (*Seated quite composedly and fondling her well-kept hands, she awaits the moment of arrival. Very soon the door opens, and the over-expected Mrs. James—a luxuriant garden of widow's weeds, enters. She is a lady more strongly and sharply featured than her sister, but there is nothing thin-lipped about her; with resolute eye and mouth a little grim, yet pleased at so finding herself, she steps into this chamber of old memories and cherished possessions, which translation to another and a better world has made hers again. For a moment she sees the desire of her eyes and is satisfied; but for a moment only. The apparition of another already in possession takes her aback.*)

JULIA (*with soft effusiveness*). Well, Laura!

LAURA (*startled*). Julia!

JULIA. *Here* you are!

LAURA. Whoever thought of finding you?

JULIA (*sweetly*). Didn't you?

> (*They have managed to embrace: but Laura continues to have her grievance.*)

LAURA.   No! not for a moment.   I really think they might have told me.   What brought you?

JULIA. ·Our old home, Laura.   It was a natural choice, I think: as one was allowed to choose.   I suppose you were?

LAURA (*her character showing*).   I didn't ask any-one's leave to come.

JULIA.   And how are you?

LAURA.   I don't know; I want my tea.

JULIA.   Hannah is just bringing it.

LAURA.   Who's Hannah?

JULIA.   *Our* Hannah: our old servant.   Didn't *she* open the door to you?

LAURA.   What?   Come back, has she?

JULIA.   I found her here when I came, seven years ago.   I didn't ask questions.   Here she is.

(ENTER *Hannah with the tea-tray.*)

LAURA (*with a sort of grim jocosity*).   How d'ye do, Hannah?

HANNAH.   Nicely, thank you, Ma'am.   How are you, Ma'am?

> (*Hannah, as she puts down the tray, is prepared to have her hand shaken: for it is a long time (thirty years or so in earthly measure) since they met. But Mrs. James is not so cordial as all that.*)

94

LAURA. I'm very tired.

JULIA. You've come a long way.

(*But Laura's sharp attention has gone elsewhere.*)

LAURA. Hannah, what have you got my best tray
for ? You know that is not to be used every day.

JULIA. It's all right, Laura. You don't understand.

LAURA. What don't I understand ?

JULIA. Here one always uses the best. Nothing
wears out or gets broken.

LAURA. Then where's the pleasure of it ? If one
always uses them and they never break—' best '
means nothing !

JULIA. It is a little puzzling at first. You must
be patient.

LAURA. I'm not a child, Julia.

JULIA (*beautifully ignoring*). A little more coal,
please, Hannah. (*Then to her sister as she pours out
the tea.*) And how did you leave everybody ?

LAURA. Oh, pretty much as usual. Most of them
having colds. That's how I got mine. Mrs. Hilliard
came to call and left it behind her. I went out with
it in an east wind and that finished me.

JULIA. Oh, but how provoking ! (*She wishes to
be sympathetic ; but this is a line of conversation she
instinctively avoids.*)

LAURA.   *No*, Julia! . . . (*This, delivered with force, arrests the criminal intention.*)   *No* sugar.   To think of your forgetting that!

JULIA (*most sweetly*).   Milk?

LAURA.   Yes, you know I take milk.

> (*Crossing over, but sitting away from the tea-table, she lets her sister wait on her.*)

JULIA.   Did Martha send me any message?

LAURA.   How could she?   She didn't know I was coming.

JULIA.   Was it so sudden?

LAURA.   I sent for her and she didn't come.   Think of that!

JULIA.   Oh!   She would be sorry.   Tea-cake?

LAURA (*taking the tea-cake that is offered her*).   I'm not so sure.   She was nursing Edwin's boy through the measles, so of course *I* didn't count.   (*Nosing suspiciously.*)   Is this China tea?

JULIA.   If you like to think it.   You have as you choose.   How is our brother, Edwin?

LAURA.   His wife's more trying than ever.   Julia, what a fool that woman is!

JULIA.   Well, let's hope he doesn't know it.

LAURA.   He must know.   I've told him.   She sent a wreath to my funeral, ' With love and fond affection, from Emily.'   Fond fiddlesticks!   Humbug!   She knows I can't abide her.

JULIA. I suppose she thought it was the correct thing.

LAURA. And I doubt if it cost more than ten shillings. Now Mrs. Dobson—you remember her: she lives in Tudor Street with a daughter one never sees— something wrong in her head, and has fits—she sent me a cross of lilies, white lilac, and stephanotis, as handsome as you could wish; and a card—I forget what was on the card. . . . Julia, when you died——

JULIA. Oh, don't Laura!

LAURA. Well, you did die, didn't you?

JULIA. Here one doesn't talk of it. That's over. There are things you will have to learn.

LAURA. What I was going to say was—when I died I found my sight was much better. I could read all the cards without my glasses. Do *you* use glasses?

JULIA. Sometimes, for association. I have these of our dear Mother's in her tortoise-shell case.

LAURA. That reminds me. Where is our Mother?

JULIA. She comes—sometimes.

LAURA. Why isn't she here always?

JULIA (*with pained sweetness*). I don't know, Laura. I never ask questions.

LAURA. Really, Julia, I shall be afraid to open my mouth presently!

JULIA (*long-suffering still*). When you see her you

G   97

will understand. I told her you were coming, so I daresay she will look in.

LAURA. 'Look in'!

JULIA. Perhaps. That is her chair, you remember. She always sits there, still.

(ENTER *Hannah with the coal.*)

Just a little on, please, Hannah—only a little.

LAURA. This isn't China tea: it's Indian, three and sixpenny.

JULIA. Mine is ten shilling China.

LAURA. Lor', Julia! How are you able to afford it?

JULIA. A little imagination goes a long way here, you'll find. Once I tasted it. So now I can always taste it.

LAURA. Well! I wish I'd known.

JULIA. Now you *do.*

LAURA. But I never tasted tea at more than three-and-six. Had I known, I could have got two ounces of the very best, and had it when——

JULIA. A lost opportunity. Life is full of them.

LAURA. Then you mean to tell me that if I had indulged more then, I could indulge more now?

JULIA. Undoubtedly. As I never knew what it was to wear sables, I have to be content with ermine.

98

LAURA. Lor', Julia, how paltry!

(*While this conversation has been going on, a gentle old lady has appeared upon the scene, unnoticed and unannounced. One perceives, that is to say, that the high-backed arm-chair beside the fire, sheltered by a screen from all possibility of draughts, has an occupant. Dress and appearance show a doubly septuagenarian character : at the age of seventy, which in this place she retains as the hall-mark of her earthly pilgrimage, she belongs also to the 'seventies' of the last century, wears watered silk, and retains under her cap a shortened and stiffer version of the side-curls with which she and all ' the sex' captivated the hearts of Charles Dickens and other novelists in their early youth. She has soft and indeterminate features, and when she speaks her voice, a little shaken by the quaver of age, is soft and indeterminate also. Gentle and lovable, you will be surprised to discover that she, also, has a will of her own ; but for the present this does not show. From the dimly illumined corner behind the lamp her voice comes soothingly to break the discussion.*)

OLD LADY. My dear, would you move the light a little nearer ? I've dropped a stitch.

LAURA (*starting up*). Why, Mother dear, when did you come in ?

JULIA (*interposing with arresting hand*). Don't! You mustn't try to touch her, or she goes.

LAURA. Goes ?

JULIA. I can't explain. She is not quite herself. She doesn't always hear what one says.

LAURA (*assertively*). She can hear me. (*To prove it, she raises her voice defiantly.*) Can't you, Mother ?

MRS. R. (*the voice perhaps reminding her*). Jane, dear, I wonder what's become of Laura, little Laura : she was always so naughty and difficult to manage, so different from Martha—and the rest.

LAURA. Lor', Julia! Is it as bad as that ? Mother, ' little Laura ' is here, sitting in front of you. Don't you know me ?

MRS. R. Do you remember, Jane, one day when we'd all started for a walk, Laura had forgotten to bring her gloves, and I sent her back for them ? And on the way she met little Dorothy Jones, and she took her gloves off her, and came back with them just as if they were her own.

LAURA. What a good memory you have, Mother ! I remember it too. She was an odious little thing, that Dorothy—always so whiney-piney.

JULIA. More tea, Laura ?

(*Laura pushes her cup at her without remark,*

> *for she has been kept waiting ; then, in loud*
> *tones, to suit the one whom she presumes*
> *to be rather deaf :)*

LAURA. Mother ! Where are you living now ?

MRS. R. I'm living, my dear.

LAURA. I said ' where ? '

JULIA. We live where it suits us, Laura.

LAURA. Julia, I wasn't addressing myself to you. Mother, where *are* you living ? . . . Why, *where* has she gone to ?

> *(For now we perceive that this gentle Old Lady*
> *so devious in her conversation has a power*
> *of self-possession, of which, very retiringly,*
> *she avails herself.)*

JULIA *(improving the occasion, as she hands back the cup, with that touch of superiority so exasperating to a near relative).* Now you see ! If you press her too much, she goes. . . . You'll have to accommodate yourself, Laura.

LAURA *(imposing her own explanation).* I think you gave me *green* tea, Julia . . . or have had it yourself.

JULIA *(knowing better).* The dear Mother seldom stays long, except when she finds me alone.

> *(Having insinuated this barb into the flesh of*
> *her ' dear sister,' she takes up her crochet*
> *with an air of great contentment. Mrs.*

*James, meanwhile, to make herself more
at home, now that tea is finished, undoes
her bonnet-strings with a tug, and lets
them hang. She is not in the best of
tempers.*)

LAURA. I don't believe she recognised me. Why
did she keep on calling me ' Jane ' ?

JULIA. She took you for poor Aunt Jane, I fancy.

LAURA (*infuriated at being taken for anyone 'poor'*).
Why should she do that, pray ?

JULIA. Well, there always was a likeness, you
know ; and you are older than you were, Laura.

LAURA (*crushingly*). Does 'poor Aunt Jane' wear
widow's weeds ? (*This reminds her not only of her own
condition, but of other things as well. She sits up and
takes a stiller bigger bite into her new world.*) Julia ! . . .
Where's William ?

JULIA. I haven't inquired.

LAURA (*self-importance and a sense of duty consuming
her*). I wish to see him.

JULIA. Better not, as it didn't occur to you before.

LAURA. Am I not to see my own husband,
pray ?

JULIA. He didn't ever live *here*, you know.

LAURA. He can come, I suppose. He has got legs
like the rest of us.

JULIA. Yes, but one can't force people : at least,

not here. You should remember that—before he married you—he had other ties.

> (*Mrs. James preserves her self-possession, but there is battle in her eye.*)

LAURA. He was married to me longer than he was to Isabel.

JULIA. They had children.

LAURA. I could have had children if I chose. I didn't choose. . . . Julia, how am I to see him ?

JULIA (*washing her hands of it*). You must manage for yourself, Laura.

LAURA. I'm puzzled ! Here are we in the next world just as we expected, and where are all the— ? I mean, oughtn't we to be seeing a great many more things than we do ?

JULIA. What sort of things ?

LAURA. Well, . . . have you seen Moses and the Prophets ?

JULIA. I haven't looked for them, Laura. On Sundays, I still go to hear Mr. Moore.

LAURA. That's you all over ! You never would go to the celebrated preachers. But I mean to. (*Pious curiosity awakens.*) What happens here, on Sundays ?

JULIA (*smiling*). Oh, just the same.

LAURA. No *High* Church ways, I hope ? If they go in for that here, I shall go out !

JULIA (*patiently explanatory*). You will go out if you wish to go out. You can choose your church. As I tell you, I always go to hear Mr. Moore; you can go and hear Canon Farrar.

LAURA. Dean Farrar, I *suppose* you mean.

JULIA. He was not Dean in my day.

LAURA. He ought to have been a Bishop—*Arch*-bishop, *I* think—so learned, and such a magnificent preacher. But I still wonder why we don't see Moses and the Prophets.

JULIA. Well, Laura, it's the world as we knew it—that for the present. No doubt other things will come in time, gradually. But I don't know : I don't ask questions.

LAURA (*doubtfully*). I suppose it *is* Heaven, in a way, though ?

JULIA. Dispensation has its own ways, Laura; and we have ours.

LAURA (*who is not going to be theologically dictated to by anyone lower than Dean Farrar*). Julia, I shall start washing the old china again.

JULIA. As you like; nothing ever gets soiled here.

LAURA. It's all very puzzling. The world seems cut in half. Things don't seem *real*.

JULIA. *More* real, I should say. We have them—as we wish them to be.

LAURA. Then why can't we have our Mother, like other things?

JULIA. Ah, with persons it is different. We all belong to ourselves now. That one has to accept.

LAURA (*stubbornly*). Does William belong to *himself*?

JULIA. I suppose.

LAURA. It isn't Scriptural!

JULIA. It's better.

LAURA. Julia, don't be blasphemous!

JULIA. To consult William's wishes, I meant.

LAURA. But I want him. I've a right to him. If he didn't mean to belong to me, he ought not to have married me.

JULIA. People make mistakes sometimes.

LAURA. Then they should stick to them. It's not honourable. Julia, I mean to have William!

JULIA (*resignedly*). You and he must arrange that between you.

LAURA (*making a dash for it*). William! William, I say! William!

JULIA. Oh, Laura, you'll wake the dead! (*She gasps, but it is too late: the hated word is out.*)

LAURA (*as one who will be obeyed*). William!

(*The door does not open; but there appears through it the indistinct figure of an elderly gentleman with a weak chin and a shifting eye. He stands irresolute and apprehensive ; clearly his presence there is perfunctory. Wearing his hat and carrying a hand-bag, he seems merely to have looked in while passing.)*

JULIA. Apparently you are to have your wish. (*She waves an introductory hand ; Mrs. James turns, and regards the unsatisfactory apparition with suspicion.*)

LAURA. William, is that you ?

WILLIAM (*nervously*). Yes, my dear ; it's **me**.

LAURA. Can't you be more distinct than that ?

WILLIAM. Why do you want me ?

LAURA. Have you forgotten I'm your wife ?

WILLIAM. I thought you were my widow, my dear.

LAURA. William, don't prevaricate. I am your wife, and you know it.

WILLIAM. Does a wife wear widow's weeds ? A widow is such a distant relation : no wonder I look indistinct.

LAURA. How did I know whether I was going to find you here ?

WILLIAM. Where else ? But you look very nice as you are, my dear. Black suits you.

(*But Mrs. James is not to be turned off by compliments.*)

LAURA. William, who are you living with ?

WILLIAM. With myself, my dear.

LAURA. Anyone else ?

WILLIAM. Off and on I have friends staying.

LAURA. Are you living with Isabel ?

WILLIAM. She comes in occasionally to see how I'm getting on.

LAURA. And how are you 'getting on '—without me ?

WILLIAM. Oh, I manage—somehow.

LAURA. Are you living a proper life, William ?

WILLIAM. Well, I'm *here*, my dear ; what more do you want to know ?

LAURA. There's a great deal I want to know. But I wish you'd come in and shut the door, instead of standing out there in the passage.

JULIA. The door *is* shut, Laura.

LAURA. Then I don't call it a door.

WILLIAM (*trying to make things pleasant*). When is a door not a door ? When it's a parent.

LAURA. William, I want to talk seriously. Do you know that when you died you left a lot of debts I didn't know about ?

WILLIAM. I didn't know about them either, my dear. But if you had, it wouldn't have made any difference.

LAURA. Yes, it would! I gave you a very expensive funeral.

WILLIAM. That was to please yourself, my dear; it didn't concern me.

LAURA. Have you no self-respect? I've been at my own funeral to-day, let me tell you!

WILLIAM. Have you, my dear? Rather trying, wasn't that?

LAURA. Yes, it was. They've gone and put me beside you; and now I begin to wish they hadn't!

WILLIAM. Go and haunt them for it!

(*At this Julia deigns a slight chuckle.*)

LAURA (*abruptly getting back to her own*). I had to go into a smaller house, William. And people knew it was because you'd left me badly off.

WILLIAM. That reflected on me, my dear, not on you.

LAURA. It reflected on me for ever having married you.

WILLIAM. I've often heard you blame yourself. Well, now you're free.

LAURA. I'm *not* free.

WILLIAM. You can be if you like. Hadn't you better?

LAURA (*sentimentally*). Don't you see I'm still in mourning for you, William?

108

WILLIAM. I appreciate the compliment, my dear. Don't spoil it.

LAURA. Don't be heartless!

WILLIAM. I'm not: far from it. (*He looks at his watch.*) I'm afraid I must go now.

LAURA. Why must you go?

WILLIAM. They are expecting me—to dinner.

LAURA. Who's ' they ' ?

WILLIAM. The children and their mother. They've invited me to stay the night.

> (*Mrs. James does her best to conceal the shock this gives her. She delivers her ultimatum with judicial firmness.*)

LAURA. William, I wish you to come and live here with me.

> (*William vanishes. Mrs. James in a fervour of virtuous indignation hastens to the door, opens it, and calls ' William!' but there is no answer.*)
>
> (*Julia, meanwhile, has rung the bell. Mrs. James stills stands glowering in the doorway when she hears footsteps, and moves majestically aside for the returned penitent to enter; but alas! it is only Hannah, obedient to the summons of the bell. Mrs. James faces round and fires a shot at her.*)

LAURA. Hannah, you *are* an ugly woman.

JULIA (*faint with horror*).   Laura !

HANNAH (*imperturbably*).   Well, Ma'am, I'm as God made me.

JULIA.   Yes, please, take the tea-things. (*Sotto voce, as Hannah approaches.*)   I'm sorry, Hannah !

HANNAH.   It doesn't matter, Ma'am. (*She picks up the tray expeditiously and carries it off.*)

(*Mrs. James eyes the departing tray, and is again reminded of something.*)

LAURA.   Julia, where is the silver tea-pot ?

JULIA.   Which, Laura ?

LAURA.   Why, that beautiful one of our Mother's.

JULIA.   When we shared our dear Mother's things between us, didn't Martha have it ?

LAURA.   Yes, she did.   But she tells me she doesn't know what's become of it.   When I ask, what did she do with it in the first place ? she loses her temper.   But once she told me she left it here with *you*.

(*The fierce eye and the accusing tone make no impression on that cushioned fortress of gentility.   With suave dignity Miss Robinson makes chaste denial.*)

JULIA.   No.

LAURA (*insistent*).   Yes ; in a box.

JULIA.   In a box ?   Oh, she may have left anything in a box.

LAURA. It was that box she always travelled about with and never opened. Well, I looked in it once (never mind how), and the tea-pot wasn't there.

JULIA (*gently, making allowance*). Well, I *didn't* look in it, Laura.

> (*Like a water-lily folding its petals she adjusts a small shawl about her shoulders, and sinks composedly into her chair.*)

LAURA. The more fool you ! . . . But all the other things she had of our Mother's *were* there : a perfect magpie's nest ! And she, living in her boxes, and never settling anywhere. What did she want with them ?

JULIA. I can't say, Laura.

LAURA. No—no more can I ; no more can anyone ! Martha has got the miser spirit. She's as grasping as a caterpillar. *I* ought to have had that tea-pot.

JULIA. Why ?

LAURA. Because I had a house of my own, and people coming to tea. Martha never had anyone to tea with her in her life—except in lodgings.

JULIA. We all like to live in our own way. Martha liked going about.

LAURA. Yes. She promised *me*, after William—I suppose I had better say 'evaporated' as you won't let me say 'died'—she promised always to stay with me for three months in the year. She never did.

Two, and some little bits, were the most. And I want to know where was that tea-pot all the time ?

JULIA (*a little jocosely*).   Not in the box, apparently.

LAURA (*returning to her accusation*).   I thought you had it.

JULIA.   You were mistaken. Had I had it here, you would have found it.

LAURA.   Did Martha never tell *you* what she did with it ?

JULIA.   I never asked, Laura.

LAURA.   Julia, if you say that again I shall scream.

JULIA.   Won't you take your things off ?

LAURA.   Presently. When I feel more at home. (*Returning to the charge.*)   But most of our Mother's things are here.

JULIA.   Your share and mine.

LAURA.   How did you get mine here ?

JULIA.   You brought them. At least, they *came*, a little before you did. Then I knew you were on your way.

LAURA (*impressed*).   Lor' ! So that's how things happen ?

> (*She goes and begins to take a look round, and Julia takes up her crochet again. As she does so her eye is arrested by a little old-fashioned hour-glass standing upon*

the table from which the tea-tray has been taken, the sands of which are still running.)

JULIA (*softly, almost to herself*). Oh, but how strange ! That was Martha's. Is Martha coming too ? (*She picks up the glass, looks at it, and sets it down again.*)

LAURA (*who is examining the china on a side-table*). Why, I declare, Julia ! Here is your Dresden that was broken—without a crack in it !

JULIA. No, Laura, it was yours that was broken.

LAURA. It was *not* mine ; it was yours. . . . Don't you remember *I* broke it ?

JULIA. When you broke it you said it was mine. Until you broke it, you said it was yours.

LAURA. Very well, then : as you wish. It isn't broken now, and it's mine.

JULIA. That's satisfactory. I get my own back again. It's the better one.

(ENTER *Hannah with a telegram on a salver.*)

HANNAH (*in a low voice of mystery*). A telegram, Ma'am.

(*Julia opens it. The contents evidently startle her, but she retains her presence of mind.*)

JULIA. No answer.

(EXIT *Hannah.*)

JULIA. Laura, Martha is coming!

LAURA. Here? Well, I wonder how she has managed that!

> (*Her sister hands her the telegram, which she reads.*)

'Accident. Quite safe. Arriving by the 6.30.' Why, it's after that now!

JULIA (*sentimentally*). Oh, Laura, only think! So now we shall be all together again.

LAURA. Yes, I suppose we shall.

JULIA. It will be quite like old days.

LAURA (*warningly, as she sits down again and prepares for narrative*). Not *quite*, Julia. (*She leans forward, and speaks with measured emphasis.*) Martha's temper has got very queer! She never had a very good temper, as you know: and it's grown on her.

> (*A pause. Julia remains silent.*)

I could tell you some things; but—— (*Seeing herself unencouraged*) oh, you'll find out soon enough! (*Then, to stand right with herself*) Julia, *am* I difficult to get on with?

JULIA. Oh well, we all have our little ways, Laura.

LAURA. But Martha: she's so rude! I can't introduce her to people! If anyone comes, she just runs away.

JULIA (*changing the subject*). D'you remember, Laura, that charming young girl we met at Mrs. Somervale's, the summer Uncle Fletcher stayed with us ?

LAURA (*snubbingly*). I can't say I do.

JULIA. I met her the other day : married, and with three children—and just as pretty and young-looking as ever.

(*All this is said with the most ravishing air, but Laura is not to be diverted.*)

LAURA. Ah ! I daresay. When Martha behaves like that, I hold my tongue and say nothing. But what people must think, I don't know. Julia, when you first came here, did you find old friends and acquaintances ? Did anybody recognise you ?

JULIA. A few called on me : nobody I didn't wish to see.

LAURA. Is that odious man who used to be our next-door neighbour—the one who played on the 'cello—here still ?

JULIA. Mr. Harper ? I see him occasionally. I don't find him odious.

LAURA. *Don't you ?*

JULIA. It was his wife who was the—— She isn't here : and I don't think he wants her.

LAURA. Where is she ?

JULIA. I didn't ask, Laura.

(*Mrs. James gives a jerk of exasperation, but at that moment the bell rings and a low knock is heard.*)

JULIA (*ecstatically*). Here she is!

LAURA. Julia, I wonder how it is Martha survived us. She's much the oldest.

JULIA (*pleasantly palpitating*). Does it matter? Does it matter?

(*The door opens and in comes Martha. She has neither the distinction of look nor the force of character which belongs to her two sisters. Age has given a depression to the plain kindliness of her face, and there is a harassed look about her eyes. She peeps into the room a little anxiously, then enters, carrying a large flat box covered in purple paper which, in her further progress across the room she lays upon the table. She talks in short jerks and has a quick, hurried way of doing things, as if she liked to get through and have done with them. It is the same when she submits herself to the embrace of her relations.*)

LAURA. Oh, so you've come at last. Quite time, too!

MARTHA. Yes, here I am.

JULIA. My dear Martha, welcome to your old home! (*Embracing her.*) How are you?

MARTHA. I'm cold. Well, Laura.

> (*Between these two the embrace is less cordial,
> but it takes place.*)

LAURA. How did you come ?

MARTHA. I don't know.

JULIA (*seeing harassment in her sister's eye*). Arrived
safely, at any rate.

MARTHA. I think I was in a railway accident, but
I can't be sure. I only heard the crash and people
shouting. I didn't wait to see. I just put my fingers
in my ears, and ran away.

LAURA. Why do you think it was a railway accident ?

MARTHA. Because I was in a railway carriage. I
was coming to your funeral. If you'd told me
you were ill I'd have come before. I was bringing
you a wreath. And then, as I tell you, there
was a crash and a shout ; and that's all I know
about it.

LAURA. Lor', Martha ! I suppose they'll have
an inquest on you.

MARTHA (*stung*). I think they'd better mind their
own business, and you mind yours !

JULIA. Laura ! Here we don't talk about such
things. They don't concern us. Would you like
!ea, Martha, or will you wait for supper ?

MARTHA (*who has shaken her head at the offer of tea,*

117

and nodded a preference for supper). You know how I've always dreaded death.

JULIA. Oh, don't, my dear Martha! It's past.

MARTHA. Yes; but it's upset me. The relief, that's what I can't get over : the relief !

JULIA. Presently you will be more used to it.

(*She helps her off with her cloak.*)

MARTHA. There were people sitting to right and to left of me and opposite ; and suddenly a sort of crash of darkness seemed to come all over me, and I saw nothing more. I didn't feel anything : only a sort of a jar here.

> (*She indicates the back of her neck. Julia finds these anatomical details painful, and holds her hands deprecatingly ; but Laura has no such qualms. She is now undoing the parcel which, she considers, is hers.*)

LAURA. I daresay it was only somebody's box from the luggage-rack. I've known that happen. I don't suppose for a minute that it was a railway accident.

> (*She unfurls the tissue paper of the box and takes out the wreath.*)

JULIA. Why talk about it ?

LAURA. Anyway, nothing has happened to these. 'With fondest love from Martha.' H'm. Pretty !

118

JULIA. Martha, would you like to go upstairs with your things ? And you, Laura ?

MARTHA. I will presently, when I've got warm.

LAURA. Not yet. Martha, why was I put into that odious shaped coffin ? More like a canoe than anything. I said it was to be straight.

MARTHA. I'd nothing to do with it, Laura. I wasn't there. You know I wasn't.

LAURA. If you'd come when I asked you, you could have seen to it.

MARTHA. You didn't tell me you were dying.

LAURA. Do people tell each other when they are dying ? They don't *know*. I told you I wasn't well.

MARTHA. You always told me that, just when I'd settled down somewhere else. . . . Of course I'd have come if I'd known ! (*testily*).

JULIA. Oh, surely we needn't go into these matters now ! Isn't it better to accept things ?

LAURA. I like to have my wishes attended to. What was going to be done about the furniture ? (*This to Martha*.) You know, I suppose, that I left it to the two of you—you and Edwin ?

MARTHA. We were going to give it to Bella, to set up house with.

LAURA. *That's* not what I intended. I meant you to keep on the house and live there. Why couldn't you ?

MARTHA (*with growing annoyance*). Well, *that's* settled now!

LAURA. It wasn't for Arabella. Arabella was never a favourite of mine. Why should Arabella have my furniture?

MARTHA. Well, you'd better send word, and have it stored up for you till doomsday! Edwin doesn't want it; he's got enough of his own.

LAURA (*in a sleek, injured voice*). Julia, I'm going upstairs to take my things off.

JULIA. Very well, Laura.

(*And Laura makes her injured exit.*)

So you've been with Edwin, and his family?

MARTHA. Yes. I'm never well there; but I wanted the change.

JULIA. You mean, you had been staying with Laura?

MARTHA. I always go and stay with her, as long as I can—three months, I'm supposed to. But this year—well, I couldn't manage with it.

JULIA. Is she so much more difficult than she used to be?

MARTHA. Of course, I don't know what she's like here.

JULIA. Oh, she has been very much herself—*poor* Laura!

MARTHA. I know! Julia, I know! And I try

to make allowances. All her life she's had her own way with somebody. Poor William! Of course I know he had his faults. But he used to come and say to me : 'Martha, I *can't* please her.' Well, poor man, he's at peace now, let's hope! Oh, Julia, I've just thought: whatever will poor William do? He's here, I suppose, somewhere?

JULIA. Oh yes, He's here, Martha.

MARTHA. She'll rout him out, depend on it.

JULIA. She has routed him out.

MARTHA (*awe-struck*). Has she?

JULIA (*shaking her head wisely*). William won't live with her ; he knows better.

MARTHA. Who will live with her, then? She's bound to get hold of somebody.

JULIA. Apparently she means to live here.

MARTHA. Then it's going to be me! I know it's going to be me! When we lived here before, it used to be poor Mamma.

JULIA. The dear Mother is quite capable of looking after herself, you'll find. You needn't belong to Laura if you don't like, Martha. I never let her take possession of *me*.

MARTHA. She seems never to want to. I don't know how you manage it.

JULIA. Oh, we've had our little tussles. But here you will find it much easier. You can vanish.

MARTHA. What do you mean ?

JULIA. I mean—vanish. It takes the place of wings. One does it almost without knowing.

MARTHA. How do you do it ?

JULIA. You just wish yourself elsewhere ; and you come back when you like.

MARTHA. Have *you* ever done it ?

JULIA (*with a world of meaning*). Not yet.

MARTHA. She won't like it. One doesn't belong to one's self, when she's about—nor does anything. I've had to hide my own things from her sometimes.

JULIA. I shouldn't wonder.

MARTHA. Do you remember the silver tea-pot ?

JULIA. I've been reminded of it.

MARTHA. It was mine, wasn't it ?

JULIA. Oh, of course.

MARTHA. Laura never would admit it was mine. She wanted it ; so I'd no right to it.

JULIA. I had a little idea that was it.

MARTHA. For years she was determined to have it : and I was determined she shouldn't have it. And she didn't have it !

JULIA. Who did have it ?

MARTHA. Henrietta *was* to. I sent it her as a wedding-present, and told her Laura was never to know. And, as she was in Australia, that seemed safe.

Well, the ship it went out in was wrecked—all because of that tea-pot, I believe! So now it's at the bottom of the sea!

JULIA. Destiny!

MARTHA. She searched my boxes to try and find it: stole my keys! I missed them, but I didn't dare say anything. I used to wrap it in my night-gown and hide it in the bed during the day, and sleep with it under my pillow at night. And I was so thankful when Henrietta got married; so as to be rid of it!

JULIA. Hush!

(RE-ENTER *Mrs. James, her bonnet still on, with the strings dangling, and her cloak on her arm.*)

LAURA. Julia I've been looking at your room in there.

JULIA (*coldly*). Have you, Laura?

LAURA. It used to be our Mother's room.

JULIA. I don't need to be reminded of that: it is why I chose it. (*Rising gracefully from her chair, she goes to attend to the fire.*)

LAURA. Don't you think it would be much better for you to give it up, and let our Mother come back and live with us?

JULIA. She has never expressed the wish.

LAURA. Of course not, with you in it.

JULIA. She was not in it when I came.

123

LAURA. How could you expect it, in a house all by herself?

JULIA. I gave her the chance: I began by occupying my own room.

LAURA (*self-caressingly*). *I* wasn't here then. That didn't occur to you, I suppose? You seem to forget you weren't the only one.

JULIA. Kind of you to remind me.

LAURA. Saucy.

JULIA. Martha, will you excuse me?

>   (*Polite to the last, she vanishes gracefully away
>   from the vicinity of the coal-box. The
>   place where she has been stooping knows
>   her no more.*)

LAURA (*rushing round the intervening table to investigate*). Julia!

>   (*Martha is quite as much surprised as Mrs.
>   James, but less indignant.*)

MARTHA. Well! Did you ever?

LAURA (*facing about after vain search*). Does she think that is the proper way to behave to *me*? Julia!

MARTHA. It's no good, Laura. You know Julia, as well as I do. If she makes up her mind to a thing——

LAURA. Yes. She's been waiting here to exercise her patience on me, and now she's happy! Well, she'll have to learn that this house doesn't belong to

124

her any longer. She has got to accommodate herself to living with others. . . . I wonder how she'd like me to go and sit in that pet chair of hers?

JULIA (*softly reappearing in the chair which the 'dear Mother' usually occupies*). You can go and sit in it if you wish, Laura.

LAURA (*ignoring her return*). Martha, do you remember that odious man who used to live next door, who played the 'cello on Sundays?

MARTHA. Oh yes, I remember. They used to hang out washing in the garden, didn't they?

LAURA (*very scandalously*). Julia is friends with him! They call on each other. His wife doesn't live with him any longer.

(*Julia rises and goes slowly and majestically out of the room.*)

LAURA (*after relishing what she conceives to be her rout of the enemy*). Martha, what do you think of Julia?

MARTHA. Oh, she's—— What do you want me to think?

LAURA. High and mighty as ever, isn't she? She's been here by herself so long she thinks the whole place is hers.

MARTHA. I daresay we shall settle down well enough presently. Which room are you sleeping in?

LAURA. Of course, I have my old one. Where do you want to go ?

MARTHA. The green room will suit me.

LAURA. And Julia means to keep our Mother's room : I can see that. No wonder she won't come and stay.

MARTHA. Have you seen her ?

LAURA. She just 'looked in,' as Julia calls it. I could see she'd hoped to find me alone. Julia always thought *she* was the favourite. I knew better.

MARTHA. How was she ?

LAURA. Just her old self ; but as if she missed something. It wasn't a *happy* face, until I spoke to her : then it all brightened up. . . . Oh, thank you for the wreath, Martha. Where did you get it ?

MARTHA. Emily made it.

LAURA. That fool ! Then she made her own too, I suppose ?

MARTHA. Yes. That went the day before, so you got it in time.

LAURA. I thought it didn't look up to much. (*She is now contemplating Emily's second effort with a critical eye.*) Now a little maiden-hair fern would have made a world of difference.

MARTHA. I don't hold with flowers myself. I think it's wasteful. But, of course, one has to do it.

LAURA (*with pained regret*). I'm sorry, Martha; I return it—with many thanks.

MARTHA. What's the good of that? I can't give it back to Emily, now!

LAURA (*with quiet grief*). I don't wish to be a cause of waste.

MARTHA. Well, take it to pieces, then; and put them in water—or wear it round your head!

LAURA. Ten beautiful wreaths my friends sent me. They are all lying on my grave now! A pity that love is so wasteful! Well, I suppose I must go now and change into my cap. (*Goes to the door, where she encounters Julia.*) Why, Julia, you nearly knocked me down!

JULIA (*ironically*). I beg your pardon, Laura; it comes of using the same door. Hannah has lighted a fire in your room.

LAURA. That's sensible at any rate.

(EXIT *Mrs. James.*)

JULIA. Well? And how do you find Laura?

MARTHA. Julia, I don't know whether I can stand her.

JULIA. She hasn't got quite—used to herself yet.

MARTHA (*explosively*). Put that away somewhere! (*She gives an angry shove to the wreath.*)

JULIA. Put it away! Why?

MARTHA (*furiously*). Emily made it: and it didn't

127

cost anything; and it hasn't got any maiden-hair fern in it; and it's too big to wear with her cap. So it's good for nothing! Put it on the fire! She doesn't want to see it again.

JULIA (*comprehending the situation, restores the wreath to its box*). Why did you bring it here, Martha?

MARTHA (*miserably*). I don't know. I just clung on to it. I suppose it was on my mind to look after it, and see it wasn't damaged. So I found I'd brought it with me. . . . I believe, now I think of it, I've brought some sandwiches, too. (*She routs in a small hand-bag.*) Yes, I have. Well, I can have them for supper. . . . Emily made those too.

JULIA. Then I think you'd better let Hannah have them—for the sake of peace.

MARTHA (*woefully*). I thought I *was* going to have peace here.

JULIA. It will be all right, Martha—presently.

MARTHA. Well, I don't want to be uncharitable; but I do wish—I must say it—I do wish Laura had been cremated.

> (*This is the nearest she can do for wishing her sister in the place to which she thinks she belongs. But the uncremated Mrs. James now re-enters in widow's cap.*)

LAURA. Julia, have you ever seen Papa, since you came here?

JULIA (*rigidly*). No, I have not.

LAURA. Has our Mother seen him?

JULIA. I haven't—— (*About to say the forbidden thing, she checks herself.*) Mamma has *not* seen him: nor does she know his whereabouts.

LAURA. Does nobody know?

JULIA. Nobody that I know of.

LAURA. Well, but he must be somewhere. Is there no way of finding him?

JULIA. Perhaps you can devise one. I suppose, if we chose, we could go to him; but I'm not sure— as he doesn't come to us.

LAURA. Lor', Julia! Suppose he should be——

JULIA (*deprecatingly*). Oh, Laura!

LAURA. But, Julia, it's very awkward, not to know where one's own father is. Don't people ever ask?

JULIA. Never, I'm thankful to say.

LAURA. Why not?

JULIA. Perhaps *they* know better.

LAURA (*after a pause*). I'm afraid he didn't lead a good life.

MARTHA. Oh, why can't you let the thing be? If you don't remember him, I do. I was fond of him. He was always very kind to us as children; and if he did run away with the governess it was a good riddance—so far as she was concerned. We hated her.

I

LAURA. I wonder whether they are together still. You haven't inquired after *her*, I suppose ?

JULIA (*luxuriating in her weariness*). I—have—*not*, Laura !

LAURA. Don't you think it's our solemn duty to inquire ? I shall ask our Mother.

JULIA. I hope you will do nothing of the sort.

LAURA. But we ought to know : otherwise we don't know how to think of him, whether with mercy and pardon for his sins, or with reprobation.

MARTHA (*angrily*). Why need you think ? Why can't you leave him alone ?

LAURA. An immortal soul, Martha. It's no good leaving him alone : that won't alter facts.

JULIA. I don't think this is quite a nice subject for discussion.

LAURA. Nice ? Was it ever intended to be nice ? Eternal punishment wasn't provided as a consolation prize for anybody, so far as I know.

MARTHA. I think it's very horrible—for us to be sitting here—by the fire, and— (*But theology is not Martha's strong point*). Oh ! why can't you leave it ?

LAURA. Because it's got to be faced ; and I mean to face it. Now, Martha, don't try to get out of it. We have got to find our Father.

JULIA. I think, before doing anything, we ought to consult Mamma.

LAURA. Very well; call her and consult her! You were against it just now.

JULIA. I am against it still. It's all so unnecessary.

MARTHA. Lor', there *is* Mamma!

(*Old Mrs. Robinson is once more in her place. Martha makes a move toward her.*)

JULIA. Don't, Martha. She doesn't like to be——

MRS. R. I've heard what you've been talking about. No, I haven't seen him. I've tried to get him to come to me, but he didn't seem to want. Martha, my dear, how are you?

MARTHA. Oh, I'm—much as usual. And you, Mother?

MRS. R. Well, what about your Father? Who wants him?

LAURA. I want him, Mother.

MRS. R. What for?

LAURA. First we want to know what sort of a life he is leading. Then we want to ask him about his will.

JULIA. Oh, Laura!

MARTHA. *I* don't. I don't care if he made a dozen.

LAURA. So I thought if we all *called* him. *You* heard when I called, didn't you? Oh no, that was William.

MRS. R. Who's William?

LAURA. Didn't you know I was married?

MRS. R.   No.   Did he die?

LAURA.   Well, now, couldn't we call him?

MRS. R.   I daresay.   He won't like it.

LAURA.   He must.   He belongs to us.

MRS. R.   Yes, I suppose—as I wouldn't divorce him, though he wanted me to.   I said marriages were made in Heaven.

A VOICE.   Luckily, they don't last there.

> (*Greatly startled, they look around, and perceive presently in the mirror over the mantel-piece the apparition of a figure which they seem dimly to recognise. A tall, florid gentleman of the Dundreary type, with long side-whiskers, and dressed in the fashion of sixty years ago, has taken up his position to one side of the ormolu clock ; standing, eye-glass in eye, with folded arms resting on the mantel-slab and a stylish hat in one hand, he gazes upon the assembled family with quizzical benevolence.*)

MRS. R. (*placidly*).   What, is that you, Thomas?

THOMAS (*with the fashionable lisp of the fifties, always substituting 'th' for 's'*).   How do you do, Susan?

> (*There follows a pause, broken courageously by Mrs. James.*)

LAURA.   Are *you* my Father?

132

THOMAS. I don't know. Who are *you* ? Who are all of you ?

LAURA. Perhaps I had better explain. This is our dear Mother : her you recognise. You are her husband ; we are your daughters. This is Martha, this is Julia, and I'm Laura.

THOMAS. Is this true, Susan ? Are these our progeny ?

MRS. R. Yes—that is—yes, Thomas.

THOMAS. I should not have known it. They all look so much older.

LAURA. Than when you left us ? Naturally !

THOMAS. Than *me*, I meant. But you all seem flourishing.

LAURA. Because we lived longer. Papa, when did you die ?

JULIA. Oh ! Laura !

THOMAS. I don't know, child.

LAURA. Don't know ? How don't you know ?

THOMAS. Because in prisons, and other lunatic asylums, one isn't allowed to know anything.

MRS. R. A lunatic asylum ! Oh, Thomas, what brought you there ?

THOMAS. A damned life, Susan—with you, and others.

JULIA. Oh, Laura, why did you do this ?

MARTHA. If this goes on, I shall leave the room.

LAURA. Where are those *others* now?

THOMAS. Three of them I see before me. You, Laura, used to scream horribly. When you were teething, I was sleepless. Your Mother insisted on having you in the room with us. No wonder I went elsewhere.

MARTHA. I'm going!

THOMAS. Don't, Martha! You were the quietest of the lot. When you were two years old I even began to like you. You were the exception.

LAURA. Haven't you any affection for your old home?

THOMAS. None. It was a prison. You were the gaolers and the turnkeys. To keep my feet in the domestic way you made me wool-work slippers, and I had to wear them. You gave me neckties, which I wouldn't wear. You gave me affection of a demanding kind, which I didn't want. You gave me a moral atmosphere which I detested. And at last I could bear it no more, and I escaped.

LAURA (*deaf to instruction*). Papa, we wish you and our dear Mother to come back and live with us.

THOMAS. Live with my grandmother! How could I live with any of you?

LAURA. Where *are* you living?

THOMAS. Ask no questions, and you will be told no lies.

LAURA. Where is *she* ?

THOMAS. Which she ?

LAURA. The governess.

THOMAS. Which governess ?

LAURA. The one you went away with.

THOMAS. D'you want her back again ? You can have her. She'll teach you a thing or two. She did *me*.

LAURA. Then—you have repented, Papa ?

THOMAS. God ! why did I come here ?

MRS. R. Yes ; why did you come ? It was weak of you.

THOMAS. Because I never could resist women.

LAURA. Were you really mad when you died, Papa ?

THOMAS. Yes, and am still : stark, staring, raving, mad, like all the rest of you.

LAURA. I am not aware that *I* am mad.

THOMAS. Then you are a bad case. Not to know it, is the worst sign of all. It's in the family : you can't help being. Everything you say and do proves it. . . . You were mad to come here. You are mad to remain here. You were mad to want to see me. I was mad to let you see me. I was mad at the mere sight of you ; and I'm mad to be off again ! Good-bye, Susan. If you send for me again, I shan't come !

(*He puts on his hat with a flourish.*)

LAURA. Where are you going, Father ?

THOMAS. To Hell, child !   Your Hell, my Heaven !

> (*He spreads his arms and rises up through the looking-glass ; you see his violet frock-coat, his check trousers, his white spats, and patent-leather boots ascending into and passing from view. He twiddles his feet at them and vanishes.*)

JULIA. And now I hope you are satisfied, Laura ?

MARTHA. Where's Mamma gone ?

JULIA. So you've driven her away, too. Well, that finishes it.

> (*Apparently it does. Robbed of her parental prey, Mrs. James reverts to the next dearest possession she is concerned about.*)

LAURA. Martha, where is the silver tea-pot ?

MARTHA. I don't know, Laura.

LAURA. You said Julia had it.

MARTHA. I didn't say anything of the sort !   You said—you supposed Julia had it ; and I said—suppose she had !   And I left it at that.

LAURA. Julia says she hasn't got it, so you *must* have it.

MARTHA. I haven't !

LAURA. Then where is it ?

MARTHA. I don't know any more than Julia knows.

136

LAURA. Then one of you is not telling the truth. . . . (*Very judicially she begins to examine the two culprits.*) Julia, when did you last see it?

JULIA. On the day, Laura, when we shared things between us. It became Martha's: and I never saw it again.

LAURA. Martha, when did you last see it?

MARTHA. I have not seen it—for I don't know how long.

LAURA. That is no answer to my question.

MARTHA (*vindictively*). Well, if you want to know, it's at the bottom of the sea.

LAURA (*deliberately*). Don't talk—nonsense.

MARTHA. Unless a shark has eaten it.

LAURA. When I ask a reasonable question, Martha, I expect a reasonable answer.

MARTHA. I've given you a reasonable answer! And I wish the Judgment Day would come, and the sea give up its dead, and then—— (*At the end of her resources, the poor lady begins to gather herself up, so as once for all to have done with it.*) Now, I am going down-stairs to talk to Hannah.

LAURA. You will do nothing of the kind, Martha.

MARTHA. I'm not going to be bullied—not by you or anyone.

LAURA. I must request you to wait and hear what I've got to say.

137

MARTHA. I don't want to hear it.

LAURA. Julia, are we not to discuss this matter, pray?

> (*Julia, who has her eye on Martha, and is quite enjoying this tussle of the two, says nothing.*)

MARTHA. You and Julia can discuss it. I am going downstairs.

> (*Mrs. James crosses the room, locks the door, and, standing mistress of all she surveys, inquires with grim humour.*)

LAURA. And where are you going to be, Julia?

JULIA. I am where I am, Laura. I'm not going out of the window, or up the chimney, if that's what you mean.

> (*She continues gracefully to do her crochet.*)

LAURA. Now, Martha, if you please.

MARTHA (*goaded into victory*). I'm sorry, Julia. You'd better explain. I'm going downstairs.

> (*Suiting the action to the word, she commits herself doggedly to the experiment, descending bluntly and without grace through the carpet into the room below. Mrs. James stands stupent.*)

LAURA. Martha! . . . Am I to be defied in this way?

JULIA. You brought it on yourself, Laura.

LAURA.   You told her to do it !

JULIA.   She would have soon found out for herself. (*Collectedly, she folds up her work and rises.*) And now, I think, I will go to my room and wash my hands for supper.

> (*As she makes her stately move, her ear is attracted by a curious metallic sound repeated at intervals. Turning about, she perceives, indeed they both perceive, in the centre of the small table, a handsome silver tea-pot which opens and shuts its lid at them, as if trying to speak.*)

JULIA.   Oh, look, Laura ! Martha's tea-pot has arrived.

LAURA.   She told a lie, then.

JULIA.   No, it was the truth. She wished for it. The sea has given up its dead.

LAURA.   Then now I *have* got it at last !

> (*But, as she goes to seize the disputed possession, Martha rises through the floor, grabs the tea-pot, and descends to the nether regions once more.*)

LAURA (*glaring at her sister with haggard eye*).   Julia, where *are* we ?

JULIA.   I don't know what you mean, Laura. (*She reaches out a polite hand.*)   The key ?

> (*Mrs. James delivers up the key as one glad to be rid of it.*)

LAURA.   What is this place we've come to?

JULIA (*persuasively*).   Our home.

LAURA.   I think we are in Hell!

JULIA (*going to the door, which she unlocks with soft triumph*).   We are all where we wish to be, Laura. (*A gong sounds.*)   That's supper.   (*The gong continues its metallic bumbling.*)

>   (*Julia departs, leaving Mrs. James in undisputed possession of the situation she has made for herself.*)

CURTAIN

Part Three

Dethronements

IMAGINARY PORTRAITS OF POLITICAL CHARACTERS,
DONE IN DIALOGUE

Preface

THE written dialogue, as interpretative of character, is but a form of portraiture, no more
personally identified with its subject than drawing
or painting; nor can it claim to have more verisimilitude until it finds embodiment on the stage.
Why then, in this country at any rate, is its applica-
tion to living persons only considered legitimate when
associated with caricature? So sponsored, in the
pages of *Punch* and the composition of Mr. Max
Beerbohm, it has become an accepted convention
too habitual for remark. Yet caricature and verbal
parody may be as critical both of personality and
character as dialogue more seriously designed, and
may have as important an influence not merely
upon a public opinion, but upon its moral judgment
as well.

The defection of *Punch* was felt by Gladstone to
be a serious set-back to the fortunes of his Home Rule
policy; and Tenniel's cartoon of "the Grand old
Janus," saying "Quite right!" to the police who
were bludgeoning an English mob, and "Quite
wrong!" to the police who were bludgeoning an Irish
one, was a personal jibe which hit him hard.

The customary device, where contemporaries are

concerned, of disembowelling the victim's name, and leaving it a skeleton of consonants, is a formal concession which in effect concedes nothing. Nor is there any reason why it should ; for the only valid objection to the medium of dialogue is in cases where its form might mislead the reader into mistaking fiction for fact, and the author's invention for the *ipsissima verba* of the characters he portrays. I hope that this book will attract no readers so unintelligent. Having chosen dialogue for these studies of historical events because I find in it a natural and direct means to the interpretation of character, my main scruple is satisfied when I have made it plain that they have no more authenticity because they happen to be written in dramatic form, than they would have were they written as political essays. These are imaginary conversations which never actually took place ; and though I think they have a nearer relation to the minds of the supposed speakers than have King's speeches to the person who utters them, they must merely be taken as a personal reading of characters and events, tributes to men for all of whom I have, in one way or another, a very great respect and admiration ; and not least for the one whom, with a reticence that is symbolical of the part he played in the downfall of " The Man of Business," I have here left nameless.

The King-maker

Note

READERS of this dialogue may need to be reminded, for clearer understanding, of the following sequence of events. On November 15th, 1890, a *decree nisi* was pronounced in the undefended divorce suit O'Shea *v*. O'Shea and Parnell. On November 24th, Gladstone, in a letter to John Morley, stated that Parnell's retention of the Irish leadership would be fatal to his own continued advocacy of the Irish cause. In December, the majority of the Irish Party threw over Parnell in order to placate the " Nonconformist conscience," and retain the co-operation of the Liberal Party under Gladstone's leadership. During the months following, Parnell and his adherents suffered a series of defeats at by-elections in Ireland. In June 1891, immediately on the *decree nisi* being made absolute, Parnell married Katharine O'Shea. On October 6th he died.

Dramatis Personæ.

CHARLES STEWART PARNELL
(Dethroned " King " of Ireland).

KATHARINE PARNELL
(His wife : divorced wife of Captain O'Shea).

A MAN
(Ex-valet to Captain O'Shea).

A SERVANT.

The King-maker

Brighton. October 1891.

*In a comfortably furnished sitting-room, with
windows looking upon the sea-parade, a Woman of
distinguished beauty sits reading beside the fire,
so intently occupied that she pays no heed to the
entry of the Servant, who unobtrusively lights the
gas, draws down the blinds, and closes the curtains.
Then taking up a tea-tray, served for two, she
retires, and the reader is left alone. But not for
long. The slam of the street-door causes an attention which the coming and going of the Servant has
failed to arouse ; and now, as the door opens, the
brightened interest of her face tells that, without
seeing, she knows who is there. Quietly, almost
furtively, she lets fall the paper she has been
reading, and turns to her husband eyes of serene
welcome, meeting confidently the sharp interrogation of his glance.*

PARNELL.   What are you doing ?

KATHARINE.   I was reading.

PARNELL.   Yes ?   What ?

KATHARINE. Those papers you just brought in.

PARNELL. And I told you not to.

KATHARINE (*smiling*). I was wilful and disobeyed.

PARNELL (*picking up the paper, and looking at it with contemptuous disgust*). Why did you?

KATHARINE. Isn't "wilful" a sufficient answer, my dear?

> (*And with a covert look of amusement she watches him tear and throw the paper into the fire.*)

Why do you try to make me a coward? You aren't one yourself.

PARNELL. That gutter-stuff! (*And the second paper joins its fellow in the flames.*)

KATHARINE. Now wasn't that just a bit unnecessary? After all, they are helping to make history. That is public opinion—the voice of the people, you know.

PARNELL. Not *our* people!

KATHARINE. Oh? Have you brought back any better news—from there?

PARNELL. Nothing special. The result of the election was out.

KATHARINE. You didn't wire it. How much were we to the bad?

PARNELL. A few hundred. What does more or less matter? It's—it's the priests who are winning now.

KATHARINE. With divided congregations as the result.

PARNELL. Yes. But I'd rather they won than the politicians. They are honest, at any rate. Poor fools!

KATHARINE. So it's the real country we are seeing now?

PARNELL. Yes. That's the material I've had to work with!

KATHARINE. Wonderful—considering.

PARNELL. And now—now one gets to the root! But I always knew it.

KATHARINE. So you are not disappointed?

PARNELL. No; only defeated. Yet I did think once that I was going to win.

KATHARINE. So you will.

PARNELL. When I'm dead, no doubt . . . some day. You can't fight for a winning cause, and not know that.

KATHARINE. But you are not going to die yet, dearest.

PARNELL (*with a deep sigh of dejection*). Oh! Wifie, I'm so tired, so tired!

KATHARINE. Well, who has a better right? Be tired, my dear! Give yourself up to it: let everything else go, and just rest! You *are* tired out. That's what I've been telling you.

PARNELL. Too much to do yet. Even dying would take more time than I can spare just now.

KATHARINE. But you must spare time to live, my dear—if you really wish to.

PARNELL. Wish ? I never wished it more—for now I *am* living. I'm awake. Doubts are over.

KATHARINE. King . . . look at me ! Don't take your eyes away, till I've done. . . . One of those papers said (what others have been saying) that it was I . . . I . . . need I go on ?

PARNELL (*with grim tenderness*). Till you've done : you said . . .

KATHARINE. I—that have ruined you.

PARNELL. That's just what they would say, of course. It's so easy : and pleases—so many.

KATHARINE. All the same—by mere accident—mayn't it be true ? It *has* happened, you know, sometimes, that love and politics haven't quite gone together.

PARNELL. Love and politics never do. Do you think I've loved any of my party-followers : that any of them have loved me ?

KATHARINE. Doesn't—O'Kelly ?

PARNELL. He's gone now—with the rest.

KATHARINE. Didn't Mr. Biggar ?

PARNELL. Dead. . . . No.

KATHARINE. Still, you love—Ireland.

PARNELL. Not as she is to-day—so narrow and jealous, so stupid, so blind ! Has she anything alive in her now worth saving ? That Ireland has got to die; and, though it doesn't sound like it, this is the death-rattle beginning. Ireland is going to fail, and deserves to fail. But another Ireland won't fail. She's learning her lesson—or *will* learn it, in the grave. Something like this was bound to come; but if it were to come again twenty years on, it wouldn't count. She'd know better.

KATHARINE. Twenty years! We shall be an old couple by then.

PARNELL. In the life of a nation twenty years is nothing. No. Ireland was shaped for failure: she has it in her. It had got to come out. Subjection, oppression, starvation, haven't taught her enough: she must face betrayal too, of the most mischievous kind—the betrayal of well-meaning fools. After that, paralysis, loss of confidence, loss of will, loss of faith—in false leaders. Then she'll begin to learn.

KATHARINE. Do you mean that everything *has* failed now?

PARNELL. Yes; if *I* fail. I'm not thinking of myself as indispensable: it's the principle. That's what I've been trying to make them understand. But they won't, they won't! Independence, defiance —they don't see it as a principle, only as an expedient. They may make it a cry, they may feel it as their right; but when to insist on it looks like losing a point in the game—then they give up the principle, to become parasites! That's what is happening now. It's the slave in the blood coming out—the crisis of the disease. That's why I'm fighting it: and will, to the death! And when—when we are

17

dead—some day : she'll come to her senses again—
and see ! Then—this will have helped.

KATHARINE. But will it ?

PARNELL. Why ? Don't you believe that Ireland
will be free some day ?

KATHARINE. I did when she chose you for her
leader.

PARNELL (*bitterly*). A dead leader, one whom she
can't hurt, may do better for her.

KATHARINE. Don't say " dead " !

PARNELL. I shan't be alive in twenty years, my
dear. And it may take all that.

KATHARINE. Without you it will take more.

PARNELL. It won't be " without me." That's
what I mean. They may beat me to-day ; but I shall
still count. Think of all Ireland's failures ! Grattan's
Parliament counts ; " Ninety-eight " counts ; Fitz-
gerald counts ; O'Connell counts ; her famines, her
emigrations, her rebellions—all count.

KATHARINE. Does Butt count ?

PARNELL. He wasn't a failure : he didn't try to do
anything. If Ireland needs more failures, to make a
case for her conviction, shall I grudge mine ? Yes,
all her failures count : they get into the blood !
Why, even the silly statues in her streets mean more
than statues can mean here. Prosperity forgets ;
adversity remembers. Even hatred has its use :
it grips, and drives men on.

KATHARINE. Did you need—hatred, to do that for you ?

PARNELL. Yes : till I got love ! . . . Reason, conviction aren't enough. Morley said a good thing the other day. The English, he said, meant well by Ireland : but they didn't mean it much.

KATHARINE. I suppose that's true of some ?

PARNELL. Quite true : and what is the most that it amounts to ? Compromise. Morley's an authority on compromise. And yet I like him : I get on with him. But he's too thick with Gladstone to be honest over this. Curious *his* having to back the conventions, eh ?

KATHARINE. Why does he ?

PARNELL. Because the political salvation of his party and its leader comes before Ireland. He means well by her : but he doesn't mean it so much as all that. Still he's the only one of them who doesn't pretend to look on me as a black sheep. He too has to work with his material. That's politics. The Nonconformist conscience means votes—so it decides him : just as the priests decide me. . . . They would decide him in any case, I mean. And so—so it goes on. . . . " Look here upon this picture, and on this " : Ireland trying to please England ; England trying, now and then, to please Ireland ! I don't know which is the more ludicrous ; but I know that both equally must fail. And they've got to see it !—and some day they will. It won't be " Home Rule " then. . . .

(So for a while he sits and thinks, his hand in hers. Then he resumes.)

My ruin ? What would my ruin matter anyway ? Put it, that the making public of our claim—our right to each other—is to be allowed by any possibility to affect the cause of a nation—the justice of that cause : doesn't that fact, if true, show that the whole basis of the political principles they have so boasted, and on which we have so blindly relied, was utterly and fantastically false and rotten ? Haven't we, providentially, given the world the proof that it needed of its own lie ?

KATHARINE. We didn't give it, my dear.

PARNELL. Well, their proof has satisfied them, anyhow : as they are acting on it. Oh ! When I see what poor, weak things nations really are—so inadequately equipped for the shaping of their own destinies—I wonder whether in truth the history we read is not the wrong history—mere side history, to which a false significance has been given, because so much blood and treasure have been expended on it, which just a little expenditure of common sense might have spared. . . . Think of all the silly accidents and blunders, in Ireland's great chapter of accidents, which have counted for so much—even in these last few years ! . . . The Phœnix Park business—an assassination, for which perhaps only a dozen men were responsible—and at once, for that one act, more suppression and hatred and coercion are directed against a whole nation : Crimes Acts, packed juries, judges without juries, arrests without charge, imprisonments without trial. So logical, isn't it? What a means for putting a foreign Government right in the eyes of the people who deny its moral authority! . . . And then—Pigott, that shallow fraud, driven to suicide by those who were at first so eager to believe him: and the exposure of his silly forgery turns elections, makes Home Rule popular! Coming by such means, would it be worth it? . . . Gladstone, honourably hoodwinking himself all those years, accepting you as our secret go-between—and you making no pretence, my dear! Oh, I suppose it was the right and gentlemanly thing for him to pretend not to know. It was also, it seems, good politics. Chamberlain knew too—must have known; for Chamberlain's no fool; and yet to his friend, the deceived husband, said nothing! It wasn't politics; not then. Now—now it's the great stroke, and Home Rule goes down under it. . . . Is that history, or is it "Alice in Wonderland"? . . . If you are my ruin now, you were also my ruin then, when you were helping me to think that I could win justice for a nation from politicians like these: win it by any means except by beating them, bringing them to their knees, making them red with the blood of a people always in revolt, till their reputation stinks to the whole world! And when they do at last climb down and accept the inevitable, then their main thought will be only how to save their own face—and make it look a little less like the defeat they know it to be!

KATHARINE. My dear, you are so tired. Do rest!

PARNELL. I *am* resting: for now—thanks to you

—I have got at the truth! Political history is a thing made up of accidents; but not so the fate of men or of nations whose will is set to be free. No accident there! That you were tied to a man you wouldn't live with, who wouldn't live with you— was an accident. But our love was no accident; it was waiting for us before we knew anything. You and I had each a star which shone at the other's birth.

KATHARINE. Your star was mine, dearest. I hadn't one of my own.

PARNELL. Well, if nations wish to be fooled, let them go to the devil their own way, not laying the blame of their own folly on others! But having got *you*—would I ever have let you go for any power under Heaven? Why (as soon as you were free) did I marry you? I knew that, politically, it was a blunder: that over there it would go against us— prove the case. Half Ireland cared nothing for the verdict of an English jury. But when we married, they had to believe it then. . . . Well, I wanted them to believe it. I know my love would have waited, had I asked her. And it wasn't—it wasn't honour, my dear; it was much more pride: for I am a proud man, that I own: and not less since I have won you.

KATHARINE. If you hadn't been proud, dearest, you would never have got my love.

PARNELL. Oh, yes, I should. Those who love, don't love for qualities good or bad. They love them in the person they love—that's all. You have qualities which I didn't care about till I found them in you. To love is to see life—new!

KATHARINE. And whole. Some day—alone by ourselves—we will!

PARNELL. Don't we already?

KATHARINE. Yes, if only—these other things didn't interfere. But I promised; so they must.

PARNELL. My dear, when they have quite broken me—they will in time—then I'll come.

KATHARINE. You promise to go right away?

PARNELL. I promise, sweetheart.

> (*Moving toward each other they are about to embrace, when the door opens, and the Servant enters carrying a card upon a tray.*)

SERVANT. If you please, sir.

> (*Parnell takes the card; there is a pause while he looks at the name.*)

PARNELL. Will you say I am engaged.

> (*The Servant goes. Parnell hands the card to his wife.*)

I don't know the man. Do you?

KATHARINE. No. And yet I seem to remember. Yes; Willie had a man-servant of that name.

> (*The Servant returns, bearing a folded note upon her tray.*)

SERVANT. If you please, sir, I was to give you this.

PARNELL (*having read the note*). Is the man still there?

SERVANT. Yes, sir.
    (*There is a pause.*)

PARNELL. Show him in.

    (*As the Servant goes he hands the note to Katharine, and watches while she reads it.*)

So—you remember him?

KATHARINE. Only the name. . . . I may have seen him, now and then.

    (*And then enters a smooth-shaven man, sprucely dressed, with the irreproachable manners of a well-trained servant. First, with a murmured apology, he bows to the lady; then, having respectfully waited till the silence becomes marked, says:*)

MAN. Good evening, sir.

PARNELL (*glancing again at the note*). You are a valet?

MAN. Yes, sir.

PARNELL. Are you wanting a place?

MAN. No, sir. I have a place.

PARNELL. Well?

MAN. That gentleman, sir—my last employer, dismissed me without a character.

24

(His reference is to the note which Parnell still holds open in his hand.)

PARNELL. Well?

MAN. That's all, sir.

PARNELL. Then what have you come here for?

MAN. To give you this, sir.

(He draws out and presents a letter, rather soiled by keeping, which has already been opened. There is a pause, while Parnell looks first at the address, then runs his eye over the contents.)

PARNELL. May I show it to—this lady?

MAN. Oh, yes, sir.

PARNELL. Whom, I take it, you recognise?

MAN. Yes, sir. *(And meeting her glance, he bows once more.)*

(Parnell hands over the letter, and while Katharine reads there is a pause.)

PARNELL. Did you bring me this expecting money for it?

MAN. No, sir.

PARNELL. I see it has a date. You could have let me have it before?

MAN. Yes, sir.

PARNELL. More than—six months ago?

MAN. More than a year ago, sir.

PARNELL. Quite so. And you did not?

L

MAN (*eyeing him steadfastly*). No, sir. I was still comfortable in his service then, sir.

PARNELL (*ironically, after a pause of scrutiny eye to eye*). I am singularly obliged to you. . . . How did you come by it, may I ask?

MAN. Well, sir, he'd been dining out, sir. Left it in his pocket—hadn't posted it.

PARNELL. I see. . . . Had your dismissal anything to do with this?

MAN. Oh, no, sir. That only happened quite recently.

PARNELL. And then—he dismissed you without a character, you say? Do you think you deserved one?

MAN. From him, sir?—yes, sir.

PARNELL (*coldly amused*). That is a good answer. Have you been put to any expense coming here?

MAN. Just my return fare, sir.

PARNELL. And were you expecting me to——?

MAN. No, sir; I could have sent it in the post, if I'd wished.

PARNELL (*surprised*). Do you mean, then, that I may keep this letter?

MAN. Yes, sir.

PARNELL. I may do what I like with it?

MAN. Just what you like, sir.

PARNELL. Thank you.

> (*After a pause of meditation he very deliber-
> ately tears up the letter and puts it into*

*the fire. Then, with rather icy polite-
ness :)*

I am much obliged to you ; and I wish you a good
evening.

> (*A little crestfallen, but with quiet self-
> possession, the man accepts the ter-
> mination of the interview.*)

MAN. Good evening, sir. (*He moves to the door.*)

PARNELL. Stop !

> (*The man turns as the other goes towards him,
> and they meet face to face.*)

You haven't given yourself a very good character,
coming here, my man ; but you might have done
worse. Anyway, you've washed your hands of it
now. Don't do things like that again.

MAN. No, sir.

> (*And as he stands hesitating, Parnell opens
> the door.*)

Thank you, sir.
> (*The man goes. Parnell closes the door after
> him, comes meditatively across, and sits
> down. There is a long pause.*)

KATHARINE. What are you—thinking ?

PARNELL. A year ago ! . . . If he had come to me
with that a year ago—what should I have done ?

KATHARINE. You would have done just the same.

PARNELL. Torn it up ? And put it in the fire ?—
I'm not so sure.

KATHARINE. But *I* am. Hadn't he the same
right as I had, to live his own life ?

PARNELL. My dear, I said "a year ago." That
means before the case came on. That would have
stopped it—for good. . . . If I had had it—I
might have been tempted.

(*Watching him, she sees him smile.*)

KATHARINE (*rather tremulously*). Are you glad—
that you didn't have it ?

PARNELL. And use it ? Yes : I am—glad !

KATHARINE (*throwing herself into his arms*). Oh,
my dear ! Why, that means everything. You're
glad ! You're glad !

PARNELL (*clasping her*). Oh, my own love, my own
dear sweet !

KATHARINE. You regret—nothing ?

PARNELL. Nothing. Haven't I made you sure of
that—yet ?

KATHARINE. Oh, my King !—my King !

(*And just then the paper in the grate kindling
into flame, he points to it.*)

PARNELL. Look ! there goes—our proof.

KATHARINE. It doesn't matter.

PARNELL. It never did.

KATHARINE. That's what I mean.

PARNELL. But, politically, it might have made a world of difference.

KATHARINE. Yes—to the world ; not to us. We wanted to be as we are, didn't we ?

PARNELL. As we are, and as we were—how long is it ?—eleven years ago. There's been no change since. When I go back to my star, I shall have found what I came for. That's what matters most. Souls either find or lose themselves—live or die. I lived : I shouldn't have done, on this earth, but for you—but for you.

(There is a pause. He sits meditating.)

KATHARINE. And of what—now ?

PARNELL. The next generation—possibly the next but one : you and I gone, and Ireland free. In this last year we may have done more for that—than we could ever have planned. We've given them a bone to bite on : and there's meat on it—real meat. And because of that, they call you my ruin, eh ? I look rather like one, I suppose, just now. But as I came home to-night, all my mind was filled with you ; and I knew that to me you were worth far more than all the rest. And then suddenly I thought—what am I worth to you ?

KATHARINE. This—that if now you told me to go —because it was for your good—I'd go—glad—yes glad that you'd made me do for you, at last, something

29

that was hard to do—for the first time, dearest, for the first time !

PARNELL (*deeply moved*). That so ? Not an accident, then, eh ?

KATHARINE (*embracing him*). Oh, my dear, my dear, my dear !

PARNELL. How true to life love makes everything ! —so clear and straight—looking back now. Through you I've learned this truth at any rate—that there are two things about which a man must never compromise—first his own soul, the right to be himself— no matter what others may think or do.

KATHARINE. And the other ?

PARNELL. His instinct, of trust or distrust, in the character of others. I hadn't any real doubt, but I compromised with instinct to gain my end : did things I didn't believe were any good—accepted the word of men I didn't trust. Home Rule itself was a compromise that I made myself accept. But I never really believed in it. For you can't limit the liberty of a nation, if it's really alive. Then came the smash— that woke me. And that I was awake at last our love came to be the proof. . . . Something different has got to be now. Ireland will have to become more real—more herself, more of a rebel than ever she has been yet. If, thirty years hence, my failure shall have helped to bring that about—an Ireland really free—then I've won. . . .

(*The words come quietly, confidently ; but it*

is the voice of an exhausted man, whose physical resources are nearly at an end. For a long time he sits quite still, holding his wife's hand, saying nothing, for he has nothing more to say. A high screen behind the couch on which they rest cuts off the gaslight ; only the firelight plays fitfully upon the two faces. Suddenly the brightness falls away, and over that foreshadowing of death, now only three days distant, the scene closes.)

The Man of Business

Dramatis Personæ

JOSEPH CHAMBERLAIN
(Ex-Minister).

JESSE COLLINGS
(His Friend).

A DISTINGUISHED VISITOR.

A NURSE.

The Man of Business

Scene: *Highbury. August* 1913.

*Between double-doors, opening from living-room to
conservatory, sits the shadow of the once great and
powerful Minister, State Secretary for the Colonies.
To the dark, sombre tones of the heavily furnished
chamber the gorgeous colours of the orchids, hanging in trails and festoons under their luminous
dome of glass, offer a vivid contrast. Yet even
greater is that which they present to the drawn
and haggard features of the catastrophically aged
man whose public career is now over. In wheeled
chair, with lower limbs wrapped in a shawl and
supported by a foot-rest, he sits bent and almost
motionless; and when he moves head or hand, it
is head or hand only, and the motion is slow,
painful, and hesitating, as though mind functioned
on body with difficulty, uncertain of its ground.
Nevertheless, when the door opens, and the small
squat figure of a very old and dear friend advances
towards him, his face lights instantly. With tender
reverence and affection the newcomer takes hold
of his hand, lifts, presses it, lays it back again.
And when he has seated himself, the Shadow speaks.*

35

CHAMBERLAIN. Well, Collings ? Well ?

JESSE COLLINGS. Well, my dear Chamberlain, how are you ? I'm a little late, I'm afraid.

CHAMBERLAIN. I hadn't noticed. Time doesn't matter to me now.

JESSE COLLINGS. No; but I like to be punctual. It's my nature.

CHAMBERLAIN. Habit. . . . Habit and nature are different things, Collings. I've been finding that out.

(*At this, for a diversion, Collings, readjusting his pince-nez, tilts his head bird-like, and takes a genial look at his friend.*)

JESSE COLLINGS. Joe, you are looking better to-day.

CHAMBERLAIN. Well, even looks are not to be despised, I suppose, when one has nothing else left.

JESSE COLLINGS. Come, come !

CHAMBERLAIN. Yes ?

JESSE COLLINGS. Nothing else left, indeed ! Don't —don't be so *down*, Chamberlain.

CHAMBERLAIN. Dear old friend ! . . . Just now you called me " Joe." You don't often do that. Why did you ?

JESSE COLLINGS. A reversion to old habits, I suppose. One does as one gets older.

CHAMBERLAIN. Yes.

JESSE COLLINGS (*genially making conversation, which he sees to be advisable*).   I was reading only the other day that, as we get on in years and begin to forget other things, our childhood comes back to us.

CHAMBERLAIN.   Yes ?

JESSE COLLINGS.   Now I wonder if that's true ?

CHAMBERLAIN.   I wonder.

JESSE COLLINGS.   Mine hasn't begun to come back to me.

CHAMBERLAIN.   You aren't old yet.

JESSE COLLINGS.   I'm over eighty.

CHAMBERLAIN.   Good for another twenty years. And once you were my senior.   We weren't quite boys together, Collings ; but we've been good friends.

JESSE COLLINGS.   Thank God for that !—Joe.

CHAMBERLAIN.   Yes, I do.   More now than I used to.

JESSE COLLINGS.   All the same, you haven't so much cause to thank Him as we have.

CHAMBERLAIN.   No ?

        (*The listless monotone makes the little old
            man fear that he is not succeeding.*)

JESSE COLLINGS.   Is my talk tiring you ?

CHAMBERLAIN.   Not at all. . . . Please go on !

JESSE COLLINGS.   I only want to say what I said

just now : Don't be down, dear friend. Your record will stand the test better than that of others. Your work is still going on ; it hasn't finished just because you are—laid up.

CHAMBERLAIN. " Laid up " is a kind way of putting it, Collins.

JESSE COLLINGS. Why, I needn't even have said that ; when here—it's *sitting* up I find you.

CHAMBERLAIN. Sitting *out*.

JESSE COLLINGS. Well, " sitting out," if you like, for the time being. But do you imagine that this phrase or that phrase (true for the moment) states the case, counts, is worth troubling about ?

CHAMBERLAIN. Do I imagine ? No, I don't. I don't imagine anything. I was never a man of imagination.

JESSE COLLINGS. You are, when you say that !

CHAMBERLAIN. No, Collings. When I've done anything, it has been because I've had it in my hands to do. . . . My hands are empty now. Some men manage to think with their heads only ; others do it —with their stomachs you might almost say. I've never been able to think properly unless I had hold of things—had them here in my hands. . . . Look at them, now ! (*With a slow, faint gesture he indicates their helplessness ; then continues :*) I was the man of business, . . . and now, I'm out of business ; so I can't think.

JESSE COLLINGS. But that business, as you call it, Chamberlain, which you made so many of us understand for the first time—I was a " Little Englander " myself, once—that's still going on.

CHAMBERLAIN (*bitterly*). Yes, it's a fine business !

JESSE COLLINGS (*startled*). Don't you still believe in it ?

CHAMBERLAIN. As a business ? Yes. But it's going to fail all the same. There's nobody to run it now.

JESSE COLLINGS. We mean to run it, Chamberlain ! You'll see !

CHAMBERLAIN. I know you do, Collings. You are loyalty itself.

JESSE COLLINGS. There are others too. I'm not the only one.

CHAMBERLAIN. You are the best of them.

JESSE COLLINGS. No, I won't admit that.

CHAMBERLAIN. Name ?

JESSE COLLINGS. The best ? Probably some one we don't yet even know. The best are still to come. Time's with us.

CHAMBERLAIN. Is it ?

JESSE COLLINGS. Don't you think so yourself ?

CHAMBERLAIN. Not now. I did once.

39

JESSE COLLINGS. You always said so.

CHAMBERLAIN. I said it as long as I believed it : till the stars in their courses turned against me. That broke me, Collings. If I could have gone on having faith in myself, I shouldn't be—as I am now.

JESSE COLLINGS. But what—what made you lose it ?

CHAMBERLAIN. Can't you guess ?

> (*Collings shakes his head, remains valiantly incredulous ; and there is a pause.*)

I saw somebody else—whose cards weren't so good —playing with a better hand. It was the hand beat me. My head's all right still, though it sleeps. But I've lost my hand. Look at it ! (*Again the gesture illustrative of defeat.*) Threw it away. You know who I mean ?

JESSE COLLINGS (*cautiously, rather reluctantly*). I suppose I do.

CHAMBERLAIN (*watching to see the effect of his news*). He's coming to-day : to see me.

COLLINGS (*surprised*). Coming here ?

CHAMBERLAIN. Yes, it's all been nicely arranged —just a call in passing. To-morrow's papers will describe it as " a pathetic meeting." Well, when a man has to meet his executioner on friendly terms, I suppose it is " pathetic " for one of them.

> (*All this is very disconcerting to poor Collings.*

40

He helps himself to a half-sentence, and stops.)

JESSE COLLINGS. Did he himself—— ?

CHAMBERLAIN. Propose it ? Oh, yes—in the most charming way possible. Isn't it amazing how a man with charm can do things that nobody else dare ? I never managed to charm anybody.

JESSE COLLINGS. You made friends—and kept them.

CHAMBERLAIN. So does he. He has been successful all round : art, politics, letters, society—he has friends in all. I've only been successful in business.

JESSE COLLINGS. My dear friend, aren't you forgetting yourself ? You came *out* of business.

CHAMBERLAIN. No, I only changed to business on a larger scale—carried it on under a bigger name. That's how I found myself. I had to make things into a business in order to make a success of them. That was my method, Collings : glorify it as much as you like. And up to a point it was good business, I don't deny. That's how we ran local politics, invented the Caucus : Corporation Street is the result. That's how we managed to run Unionism : made a hard and fast contract of it, and made them stick to it. That's how I ran the Colonies—and the Boer War. That's how I was going to run the Empire on a Preferential Tariff. That came just too late. I'd made a mistake.

JESSE COLLINGS. What mistake ?

CHAMBERLAIN. Collings, the Boer War wasn't good

business. It might have been; but it lasted too long. Any modern war that isn't over in six months now is a blunder, you'll find. They were able to hold out too long. That did for me. There have been bees in my bonnet ever since—all because of it. Boers first; then Bannerman; then—Balfour. Just once my business instinct betrayed me, and I was done!

JESSE COLLINGS. But—wasn't the war necessary?

CHAMBERLAIN. To put the " business " on a sound footing? Yes, I thought so; it looked like it. No, it wasn't! But before I quite knew, there'd come a point where we couldn't go back; and so we just had to go on—and on. D'you know what was the cleverest thing said or done during that war? . . . You'd never guess . . . but it's true. Campbell-Bannerman's " methods of barbarism " speech. We downed him for it at the time, but it caught on—it stuck. And it was on the strength of it (with C.-B. as their hope for the future) that the Boers were persuaded to make peace: saved our face for us. They might have gone on, till we got sick of it, and the world too.

JESSE COLLINGS. I don't—I can't think you are right, Chamberlain. You are forgetting things.

CHAMBERLAIN. No—I've had difficulty about thinking so myself; but it has come to me.

(*And so he sits and meditates over the point in his career where as a business man he first failed. Presently he resumes:*)

When two men, whose qualifications I used rather to despise, beat me at business, Collings—it was a facer!

JESSE COLLINGS. Bannerman; and—the other?

CHAMBERLAIN. Comes to see me to-day. But it won't be a business meeting. He'll not say anything about it—if he can help.

JESSE COLLINGS. And you?

CHAMBERLAIN. Perhaps I shall succumb to his charm. I've done so before now.

JESSE COLLINGS. Have you and he—had words ever?

CHAMBERLAIN. Differences of opinion, of course. "Words"? How should we? He was always so wonderfully accommodating, so polite, so apologetic even. Nobody ever had a finer contempt for his party than he—not even old Dizzy, or Salisbury, or Churchill. So he could always say the handsome thing to one—behind its back—even when he was making burnt-offerings to its prejudices.

JESSE COLLINGS. And when you left him?

CHAMBERLAIN. When I left him he did the thing beautifully. So genuinely sorry to lose me; so sure of having me with him again, before long. How could I have gone out and worked against him after that? But it's what—as a business politician—I ought to have done.

JESSE COLLINGS. If you had—should we have won, straight away?

CHAMBERLAIN. We should have won the party,

43

and the party-machine too. For the rest it wouldn't have mattered waiting a year or two. Yes, we should have won. But here's this, Collings: we should have won then; we shan't win now. Times are changing: the time for it is over. Something else is coming along—what, I don't know. My old fox-scent has gone: wind's against me. The Colonies are growing up too fast. They won't separate, but they mean to stand on their own feet all the same: in their own way—not mine. We ought to have got them when they were a bit younger: we could have done it then. Once it flattered them to be called " Dominions " ; now they are going to be " Sovereign States." And he—he doesn't mind. He is never for big constructive ideas—only for contrivances : takes things as they come, makes the best of them—philosophically—and gets round them ; and sometimes does it brilliantly.

JESSE COLLINGS. What will he talk about ?

CHAMBERLAIN. Anything that comes into his head : the weather, the garden, the greenhouses, the theatres. He'll tell me, perhaps, of a book or two that I ought to read, that he hasn't had time for. He'll say, as you said, that I'm looking better than he expected. He'll say something handsome about Austen—quite genuinely meaning it. Then he'll say he's afraid of tiring me ; then he'll go. . . . Have you noticed how he shakes hands ? He hasn't much of a hand—not a real hand—but he does it, like everything else, charmingly.

44

JESSE COLLINGS (*a little crestfallen*). I thought you really liked him.

CHAMBERLAIN. So I do. Because he has beaten me, is that any reason for hating him ? If it were— after a lifetime of polls and politics, one would have to be at hate with half the world. No, from his point of view he had to beat me, and he has done it. What I stick at is that he has proved the better business man ! As I used head and hand—and heart (*and* heart, Collings !)——

JESSE COLLINGS. Yes, yes, I know you did.

CHAMBERLAIN. Some people thought I hadn't a heart : " hard as nails " they called me. . . . Well, as I used those, so he used his defeats, his doubts, his indecision, his charm—and left his heart out. That was the real business-stroke. That did for me. . . . I liked him : he knew it. Whether he ever liked me, to this day, I don't know—for certain. If he did, it made no difference. That's what I call business.

JESSE COLLINGS (*warmly*). But you've always been honourable.

CHAMBERLAIN. So has he. Don't be sentimental, Collings ! But some men manage in public life to give you a certain view of their character : so that you count on it. And then, on occasion, they play another—and get wonderful results. If I'd had that gift, I should have used it and done better. He has used it, and he has done better. I don't whine about it. But I'd rather, Collings (I suppose I'm prejudiced),

45

I'd rather he hadn't asked himself here—just now:
not just now.

> (*There is a pause, and Collings feels that he
> must say something; but finding nothing
> of any value to say, he merely commentates
> with a query.*)

JESSE COLLINGS. What has "just now" to do
with it?

CHAMBERLAIN. "Just now," dear Collings, only
means the next few months or so—possibly a year.
That's all. I had rather he'd waited, and then just
sent a wreath with the right sort of inscription on it.
He could have done that charmingly too. And I
haven't got wreaths here for *him*, for I don't think
that even a posy of these would really interest him.

> (*And with a weary gesture he points to the
> orchids, as though they were things of
> which, not impossibly, "posies" might
> be made.*)

JESSE COLLINGS (*a little perplexed by this introduction
of wreaths and flowers into political affairs*). What
does really interest him? He's so interesting
himself.

CHAMBERLAIN. You've hit it, Collings. It's himself.
Not selfishly. He stands for so many things that he
values—that he thinks good for the world—necessary
for the stability of the social order. He is their
embodiment: he is the most emblematic figure in
the modern world that I know—in this country, at
any rate—representing so much that is good in the
46

great traditions which have got to go. And to stave off that day he will do almost anything. He would even—if he thought it would enable him the better to prick some of his bubbles—he would even take office under Lloyd George.

> (*At this point, unobtrusively, a Nurse enters and stands waiting.*)

JESSE COLLINGS. I don't think we shall live to see that !

CHAMBERLAIN. I shall not ; you may.

JESSE COLLINGS (*impulsively*). Chamberlain, I don't want to live after you !

CHAMBERLAIN (*cajolingly*). Oh, yes, you do ! Anyway—I want you to. You will send me a wreath that will be worth having.

> (*Whereat his quaint little companion leans forward, and, putting his two hands pleadingly on the swathed knees, wants to speak but cannot. Slowly the sick man lets down his own and covers them. And so, hand resting on hand, he continues speaking :*)

Say what you like about the business man—the man who failed : he has known how to make friends— good ones. And you, Jesse Collings, have been one of the best : I couldn't have had a better. There's someone been waiting behind you to give you a hint that you are tiring me—staying too long. But you haven't : you never have. Perhaps, in the future, I shan't see enough of you ; perhaps, from now on,

47

my doctor will have to measure even my friends for me : three a day before meals. But I shall get life in bits still—as long as you are allowed to come. . Yes, Nurse, you make take him away now !

> (*Jesse Collings rises, and stands by his friend with moist eyes.*)

JESSE COLLINGS. Good-bye, my dear Joe, and— God bless you.

CHAMBERLAIN. Yes . . . good-bye !

> (*Hands press and part, and Jesse Collings tip-toes meekly out, apologising for the length of his stay by the softness of his going. Chamberlain's head drops, his face becomes more drawn, his hands more rigid and helpless. Without a word, his Nurse arranges his pillows, preparing him for the sleep to which his unresisting body gradually succumbs.*)

*   *   *

> (*Two hours later he is awake again, and the Nurse is removing a tray from which he has just taken some nourishment. He lifts his head and looks at her. At this sign that he is about to speak, she pauses. Presently the words come.*)

CHAMBERLAIN. Is he in there, waiting to see me ?

NURSE. Yes, sir.

CHAMBERLAIN. Ask him to come in.

NURSE. You want to see him alone, sir ?

> (*There is a pause.*)

48

CHAMBERLAIN. I think only one at a time is enough—better for me: don't you?

NURSE. It would be less tiring for you, sir.

CHAMBERLAIN. Yes. Ask him to come in.

> (*So that being settled, she goes, and he sits waiting. The afternoon sunlight is making the orchids look more resplendently themselves than ever. So still, so vivid, so alive, they hang their snake-like heads in long pendulous clusters; and among them all there is not a single one which shows the slightest sign of falling-off or decay. Presently the door is softly opened, and the Nurse, entering only to retire again, ushers in the Distinguished Visitor, whose brow, venerable with intellect, and grey with the approach of age, crowns a figure still almost youthful in its elasticity and grace, and perfect in the deliberate ease and deportment of its entry into a situation which many would find difficult. As he approaches the wheeled chair, the kindness, modesty, and distinction of his bearing prepare the way before him, and his silence has already said the nicest of nice things, in the nicest possible way, before he actually speaks. This he does not do till he has already taken and held the hand which the other has tried to offer.*)

49

DISTINGUISHED VISITOR. My dear Chamberlain, how very good of you to let me come ?

CHAMBERLAIN. Not too much out of your way, I hope ?

DIST. V. On the contrary, I could wish it were more, if that might help to express my pleasure in seeing you again.

CHAMBERLAIN. Well, what there is of me, you see. You are looking well.

DIST. V. And you—much better than I expected.

CHAMBERLAIN. Did you expect anything ?

DIST. V. I was told that you had bad days occasionally, and were unable to see anybody. I hope I am fortunate, and that this is one of your good ones ?

CHAMBERLAIN. Well, as they've let you see me, I suppose so. I don't find much difference between my good and bad days. (Won't you sit down ?) I'm still in the possession of my faculties; I sleep well, and I don't have pain.

DIST. V. (*seating himself*). And my staying with you for a little is not going to tire you ?

CHAMBERLAIN. It's far more likely to tire you, I'm afraid.

DIST. V. No, indeed not ! Apart from anything else it is a welcome respite on the journey. Motoring bores me terribly.

CHAMBERLAIN. Then you had really meant coming this way, in any case ?

DIST. V. I had been long intending to ; and when,

last week, Hewell proposed itself, all fitted together perfectly.

CHAMBERLAIN. Are they having a house-party?

DIST. V. I think not: I trust not. No, I believe a hint was dropped to them that it wasn't to be— that I was feeling far too stale for any such mental relaxation.

CHAMBERLAIN. Are you? You don't look like it.

DIST. V. In politics one tries not to look like anything; but how at the end of the session can one be otherwise?

CHAMBERLAIN. Is all going on there—as usual?

DIST. V. Yes . . . yes. I don't find being in opposition makes as much difference as I expected, as regards work. One misses the permanent official who always did it for one. Wonderful creatures— who first invented them? Pitt, or was it Pepys? Oh, no, he was one of them. A product, perhaps, of the seventeenth century.

CHAMBERLAIN. In Tudor times Prime Ministers were permanent, weren't they?

DIST. V. Their heads weren't. Executions took the place of elections in those days. And there's something to be said for it.

CHAMBERLAIN. Yes. There was more dignity about it; it gave a testimonial of character; the other doesn't.

DIST. V. Still, electoral defeat is very refreshing. Rejection by one's own constituents is sometimes a blessing in disguise: it saves one from undue familiarity. . . . That has never happened to you, has it ?

CHAMBERLAIN. It depends what one means by—constituents. In the strict sense—no.

> (*And now there is a pause, for something has been said that is not merely conversation. Very charmingly, and with a wonderful niceness of tone, the Distinguished Visitor accepts the opening that has been given him.*)

DIST. V. Chamberlain, I have been wanting to come and see you for a long time.

CHAMBERLAIN. Thank you. So I—guessed.

DIST. V. I wrote to you—a letter which you did not answer. Perhaps it did not seem to require an answer. But I hoped for one. So, after not hearing, I made up my mind to come and see you.

CHAMBERLAIN. That was very kind of you.

DIST. V. No, it wasn't ; it was natural. We've worked together—so long. And I wanted to assure myself that there was, personally—that there is now—no cloud between us ; no ill-feeling about anything. If I thought that remotely possible, I should regret it more than I can say. Speaking for myself——

CHAMBERLAIN. If you had not thought it possible—should you have come ?

DIST. V. I cannot conceive how that would have made any difference.

CHAMBERLAIN. Still, if you had not thought it possible, you would hardly have asked the question.

52

DIST. V.   Well, now I have asked it.   Speech is an overrated means of communication—especially between friends ; but it has to serve sometimes.   And you, at least, Chamberlain, have never used it as—Talleyrand, was it not ?—recommended that it should be used—for concealment.

CHAMBERLAIN.   So you think that—in words at any rate—I've been honest ?

DIST. V.   I should say pre-eminently.

CHAMBERLAIN.   And—loyal ?

DIST. V.   I have never had differences—political divergences—with any man more loyal than you, Chamberlain.

CHAMBERLAIN.   Thank you.   I value that—from you.   So the question's answered.   On my side there is no cloud, as you tell me I have nothing with which to reproach myself.

DIST. V.   Thank you for the reassurance.   In that case the heavens are clear.

CHAMBERLAIN.   I hope they are properly grateful. Such a testimonial—from two men looking in opposite directions—is an embracing one.

DIST. V.   Opposite ?   Oh, I had hoped—though we may not see eye to eye in everything—that still, in the main, we were in general agreement.

CHAMBERLAIN.   Possibly.   I daresay " a half-sheet of note-paper " might still cover our " general agreement," so long as we only talked about it.   That served us for—two years, did it not ?   But I wasn't meaning—as to our political opinions.   I meant that

53

you are still looking to the future ; I can only look back.

DIST. V.   That, for you, must be a retrospect of deep satisfaction.   It has made much history.

CHAMBERLAIN.   Catastrophes make history—sometimes.

DIST. V.   You helped to avert them.

CHAMBERLAIN.   Yes, for a time.   But another may be coming, and I shan't be here then.   And if I were, I should be no use.

DIST. V.   Oh, don't say that !   Nor can I agree, either.   No use ?   Your good word is a power we still depend on.   No, Chamberlain, we cannot do without you.

CHAMBERLAIN.   You did—when you accepted my resignation.

DIST. V.   For a fixed and an agreed purpose.   In a way that only bound us more closely.

CHAMBERLAIN.   I thought so then.   But it has turned out differently.

DIST. V.   Has it ?   I should not have said so.   Am I not to count on you still ?

CHAMBERLAIN.   As a diminishing force ?   Yes ; I shan't disappoint you.

DIST. V.   Oh !   (*Deprecatingly, as of something that need not have been said.*)   But not that at all !

CHAMBERLAIN (*rubbing it in*).   Necessarily : one who, as I said, can only look backward.   Forward, I am nothing. Believe me, I have measured myself at last. This is no miscalculation—like the other.

DIST. V. The other ?

CHAMBERLAIN. My resignation.

DIST. V. Was that one ?

CHAMBERLAIN. It certainly had not the effect I intended.

DIST. V. Surely you were not then intending to force me against my own judgment ?

CHAMBERLAIN. No ; but I thought you, and the rest, would follow.

DIST. V. I think we did : I think we still do. But sometimes, with followers, following takes time.

CHAMBERLAIN. It will take more than my time. That is where I miscalculated.

DIST. V. But, my dear Chamberlain—if one may be personal—you are maintaining your strength, are you not ? The doctors—are hopeful ?

CHAMBERLAIN. The regulation paragraphs are supplied to the papers, if that's what you mean.

DIST. V. But I had this from members of your own family.

CHAMBERLAIN. Quite so ; it is they who supply them.

DIST. V. Then, if the source is so authoritative, surely it must be true.

CHAMBERLAIN. Are newspaper paragraphs in such cases—ever true ?

DIST. V. Perhaps I am no judge. As you know, I seldom read them.

CHAMBERLAIN. Aren't the probabilities that they will always overstate the case—as far as possible?

DIST. V. That is a course which, as an old politician, —speaking generally—I must own has its advantages. So often, when things are uncertain, one has to act as if one were sure.

CHAMBERLAIN. Yes, you've done that—sometimes. Sometimes you haven't. I shouldn't call you an old politician, though. Being old is the thing you've always managed to avoid. And yet, you've been in at a good many political deaths first and last.

DIST. V. That, in itself, is an ageing experience.

CHAMBERLAIN. Yes? . . . I wonder.

DIST. V. Oh, but surely!

CHAMBERLAIN. I wasn't sure; but I take your word for it.

DIST. V. In politics, somehow, the deaths seem always to exceed the births: those who go have become more intimate: one has got to know them. Yes, the departures do certainly overshadow the arrivals.

CHAMBERLAIN. Yet sometimes they must have come to you as a relief.

DIST. V. My dear Chamberlain, don't say that! It isn't true.

CHAMBERLAIN. Oh! I wasn't thinking of myself just then.

DIST. V. You were thinking, then, of somebody?

CHAMBERLAIN. Yes, I was. I was thinking of George Wyndham. What a beautiful fellow he was! so clever, so handsome, so charming: a man cut out for success, by the very look of him. And then, all at once, down and out: the old pack had got him! How they hunted him! "Devolution!" Wouldn't they be glad to get that now?

DIST. V. At the time it was impossible.

CHAMBERLAIN. Yes, you accepted that, I know. . . . It broke his heart. . . . Did you go and see him—when he was dying?

DIST. V. I used to go and see him when I could— yes, frequently; we had been great friends. Not immediately—a month or two before, was the last time, I think.

CHAMBERLAIN. And so with him, too, you could say that you remained friends to the last! You have had a wonderful career: friends, enemies, they all loved you. Gladstone (who hadn't as a rule much love for his political opponents) made an exception in your case.

DIST. V. Yes, I owed a great deal to his generous friendship. It gave me confidence.

CHAMBERLAIN. Harcourt, too, always spoke of you with affection.

DIST. V. Oh, yes; we had a brotherly feeling about Rosebery, you know.

CHAMBERLAIN (*ignoring his diversion*). Randolph hadn't though. He was bitter.

N

DIST. V. Randolph was a performer who just once exceeded his promise, and then could never get back to it. That was his tragedy. Strange how, when he lost his following, his brilliancy all went with it.

CHAMBERLAIN. Yes, it was strange, in one so independent of others. He had a great faculty, at one time, for not caring, for being (or seeming) ruthless. It's a gift that a politician must envy. It hasn't been my way to lose my heart in politics : it's not safe. But—you charmed me.

> (*There is an implication here that the quiet tone has not obscured. And so the direct question comes :*)

DIST. V. Chamberlain, I must ask. What is there between us ?

CHAMBERLAIN. Nothing—nothing now at all—or very little.

DIST. V. No, no ; you are too sincere to pretend to misunderstand me like that.

CHAMBERLAIN. In politics can one afford to be quite—sincere ? Openly, I mean ?

DIST. V. You have been—far more than others I could name.

CHAMBERLAIN. That is a friendly judgment. Others wouldn't say so. If a man stays in politics till he ceases to be important, while others remain important, there's bound to be a change of relations.

DIST. V. In our case I don't admit that it has happened.

CHAMBERLAIN. Don't you ? You were our party-leader. I broke away ; so you had to break me. From your point of view you were right. I thought I knew the game better than you. I made a mistake.

DIST. V. Do you mean, then, that you intended to break *me* ?

CHAMBERLAIN. Oh, no. But I meant to—persuade you.

DIST. V. My view is that you did—very thoroughly. Surely I went a long way—conceded a great deal.

CHAMBERLAIN. " Half a sheet of note-paper " was the measure of it. Yes, that speech was a great success, and you remained our leader. But your halving of that sheet was the beginning of—my defeat, your victory.

DIST. V. I don't recognise either. At this moment we are both defeated, in a sense : out of office, that is to say.

CHAMBERLAIN. Yes, but you will come back. I shan't.

DIST. V. But—in all its essentials—what you stand for will.

CHAMBERLAIN. As a hang-fire, perhaps, while parties temporise and readjust themselves to a new balance. But never the same thing again. The time for it has gone. I missed it.

DIST. V. You mustn't be depressed, Chamberlain. Great policies, new orientations, need careful nursing—testing too. Conditions are changing very rapidly.

CHAMBERLAIN. Mine are getting worse. I have two nurses now—night and day : and I obey orders.

DIST. V. You do well to remind me. You shouldn't have let me tire you.

(And so saying he rises.)

CHAMBERLAIN. You don't. You used to, now and then, when we didn't agree. You had the deliberate mind, your own fixed rate of progression : one couldn't hurry you. And your semitones, and semicircles, and semi-quavers used sometimes to worry me, I own. They don't now : having become a monotone myself, I acquiesce. *I'm* the slow one, now : you've set me my pace. . . . Here I sit, stock still.

DIST. V. *(lightly diverting the conversation from its impending embarrassment).* With your old associates still round you, I see !

(And he touches a trail of blossom admiringly, as he continues :)

They, at least, in their reflected glory, look flourishing ; for they, too, have had a share in your career, have they not ?

CHAMBERLAIN. Yes, they helped me to get into *Punch*, I suppose, if not into Parliament. Yet, I never thought of it, till it happened—'twas a mere accident. Would you like to take one with you ?

DIST. V. I don't usually so efface myself, but I will with pleasure. This one is quite exquisite. May I? Thanks (*and the glory of it goes to his button-hole*). I notice, too, that it has a scent.

CHAMBERLAIN. Yes, that is a new kind, hard to rear. There are very few of it in England yet, and nowhere growing so well as they do here.

DIST. V. That is so like you, Chamberlain—you are the born expert; everything you touch—it's in your blood. Whatever you have done, you have done successfully.

CHAMBERLAIN. So I have your word for it. I was saying to Collins this morning that as a type of the really successful man you had beaten me.

DIST. V. I—a type of success? My dear Chamberlain! In my wildest dreams, I aim only at safety; and if my hesitations have sometimes distressed you, they have been far more distressing to myself. You yourself, in a moment of friendly candour, once described me (so I was told) as the champion stick-in-the-mud.

CHAMBERLAIN. So I did, and it's true. But I said "champion." If you hadn't been such a champion at it, the mud would have swallowed you up alive. Instead of that, you have made it a tower of defence against your enemies. That's why I regard you not only as so successful, but so British.

DIST. V. May I, at least, claim that even for self-defence I have not slung it at my opponents?

CHAMBERLAIN. No. Why waste it? It's your use, not your misuse of it that I so admire. If you hadn't been such a wonderful politician, you might have been a great statesman.

DIST. V. Doesn't that rather indicate failure?

CHAMBERLAIN. No. Sometimes the political world has no use for statesmen—except to down them. Sometimes it prefers politicians, and perhaps rightly. Every age makes its own peculiar requirements; and those who find out when the political line is the better one to follow, are the successful ones. You and I have been—politicians; let's be honest and own it. And now my particular politics are over. Circumstances have emptied me out. That's different from mere failure. Great statesmen have been failures; we've seen them go down, you and I— too big, too far-seeing for their day. But they went down *full*, with all the weight of their great convictions and principles still to their credit. I'm empty. Time has played me out. That's the difference.

DIST. V. I am confident that history will give a different verdict.

CHAMBERLAIN. Will it? When exactly does history begin to get written? Is a man's reputation for statesmanship safe, even after a hundred years? What about Pitt? Can one be so sure of him now? His European policy may have been a blunder; his great work in Ireland may yet have to be reversed.

DIST. V. In reversed circumstances, that may

become logical. But what has held good for a hundred year, I should incline to regard as statesmanship.

CHAMBERLAIN. "Held good"? Fetters a man can't break "hold good"; but they make a prisoner of him all the same. Policies have done that to nations before now. But would you, on that score, say of them that they have held good?

DIST. V. But let me understand, my dear Chamberlain, what exactly in Pitt's policy you now question?

CHAMBERLAIN. Nothing: I can't see far enough ahead to question anything. I only say, when does history begin to get written? We don't know.

DIST. V. What more can one do than direct it for the generation in which one lives? That, it seems to me, is our main responsibility.

CHAMBERLAIN. Well, that's what you and I have done. How? Mainly by pulling down bigger men than ourselves. Randolph, Parnell, Gladstone—we got the better of them, didn't we? Have you never wondered why men of genius get sent into the world —only to be defeated? Gladstone was a bigger man than the whole lot of us; but we pulled him down— and I enjoyed doing it. Parnell, for all his limitations, was a great man. Well, we got him down too. And I confess that gave me satisfaction. You helped to pull Randolph down; but you didn't enjoy doing it. That's where you and I were different.

DIST. V. I helped?

63

CHAMBERLAIN. Yes; it had to be done. And you were sorry for him while you did it—just as you were sorry for Wyndham.

DIST. V. But I did nothing!

CHAMBERLAIN. Quite so. He came down here to fight us in the Central division, and the Conservatives were keen for it. It was touch and go : Unionists were not in such close alliance then ; he might have succeeded. You did nothing ; wouldn't back him. (Quite right, from my point of view.) Randolph went down : never the same man again.

DIST. V. But, my dear Chamberlain, we had our agreed compact.

CHAMBERLAIN. An official understanding, certainly. But that didn't prevent me from going to the Round-Table conference. That also was touch and go ; it might have succeeded. Where would our compact have been, then ?

DIST. V. The Round-Table was merely an interrogation covering a forlorn hope. It failed because you remained loyal to your convictions.

CHAMBERLAIN. It failed because one day two of us lost our tempers—one bragged, the other bullied. That was the real reason. If Gladstone had given me a large enough hand over his first Bill, d'you suppose I shouldn't have been a Home Ruler ? I was to begin with, remember.

DIST. V. Standing for a very different Bill, I imagine.

CHAMBERLAIN. Which you would still have opposed. But I should have won.

DIST. V. Certainly, if we had lost you, it would have made a difference

CHAMBERLAIN. I was younger then : I'd more push in me. But you would have let me go, all the same. Yes, I've always admired your courage when the odds were against you. . . . So, when the time for it came, you pulled me down too. It had to be done. . . . And here I am.

DIST. V. My dear Chamberlain, you distress me deeply !

CHAMBERLAIN. Of course I do. D'you think I haven't distressed myself too ? Do I look like a man who hasn't been through anything ?

DIST. V. Then—there is a cloud between us, after all.

CHAMBERLAIN. No. I see you clearly ; I see myself clearly. There's no cloud about it ; it's all sharp, and clear, and hard—hard as nails. And I've been able to put it into words—that now you understand. Poor Randolph ! Do you remember how his tongue stumbled, and tripped him, the last time he spoke in the House ? And I saw you looking on, pitying him. You'd got a kind side to you, for all your efficiency. Men like you for that—that charm. . . . It's been a great asset to you. Parnell, how he tried all his life to make a speech and couldn't. But what he said didn't matter—there was the man !

What a force he might have been—was! What a
Samson, when he pulled the whole Irish Party down—
got them all on top of him to pull with him. What
d'you think he was doing then? Trying to give his
Irish nation a soul! It looked like pride, pique,
mere wanton destruction; but it was a great idea.
And if ever they rise to it—if ever the whole Irish
nation puts its back to the wall as Parnell wanted it to
do then—shakes off dependence, alliance, conciliation,
compromise, it may beat us yet! They were afraid
of defeat. That's why we won. A cause or a nation
that fears no defeat—nor any number of them—
that's what wins in the long run. But does any such
nation—any such cause exist? I'm not sure. . . .
I'm not really sure of anything now, only this: that
it's better not to live too long after one has failed.
To go on living then—is the worst failure of all.

> (*As he thus talks himself out, his auditor's
> solicitous concern has continually in-
> creased; and now when, for the first time,
> the voice breaks with exhaustion and
> emotion, the other, half-rising from his
> seat, interposes with gentle but insistent
> urgency.*)

DIST. V. My dear Chamberlain, you are overtaxing
your strength; you are doing yourself harm. You
ought not to go on. Stop, I do beg of you!

CHAMBERLAIN. Stop? Why stop? What does it
matter now?

> (*But even as he speaks, mind and will cease
> to contest the point where physical energy*

*fails. His manner changes, his voice
becomes dull and listless of tone.)*

Oh, yes . . . yes. You are quite right. It's
time. I'm under orders now. Would you mind—
the bell ?

> *(Then, as the other is about to rise, he perceives
> that the Nurse has already entered, and
> now stands, unobtrusive but firm, awaiting
> the moment to reassert her sway.)*

Oh, it's not necessary. There's the Nurse come
again, to remind me that I mustn't tire myself in
tiring you.

> *(And so, under the presiding eye of professional
> attendance, the Visitor rises and advances
> to take his leave.)*

Thank you—for coming. Thank you—for hearing
me so patiently. . . . You always did that, even
though it made no difference. . . . I wonder—shall
I ever see you again ?

DIST. V.   You shall. I promise.

CHAMBERLAIN.   I wonder.

DIST. V.   I assure you, I shall make a point of it.
Believe me, I am very grateful for this opportunity
you have given me ; and even more am I grateful
for all your long loyalty in the past. Through all
differences, through all difficulties, I have felt that
you were indeed a friend. So, till we meet again, my
dear Chamberlain, good-bye !

> *(The two hands meet and part, while the Nurse
> moves forward to resume her professional*

duties. *The Distinguished Visitor begins
to retire.*)

CHAMBERLAIN. Good-bye. . . . You can find
your way ?

DIST. V. (*turning gracefully as he goes*). Perfectly !
(*And treating the door with the same perfection
of courtesy as he treats all with whom he
comes in contact, he goes to take his leave
of other members of the family. The door
closes ; the Nurse is punching the pillows ;
Chamberlain speaks :*)

CHAMBERLAIN. So that's the end, eh ? . . .
Charming fellow !
(*And so saying, he settles back to the inatten-
tion of life to which he has become
accustomed.*)

The Instrument

Dramatis Personæ

WOODROW WILSON
  (*Ex-President of the United States of America*).

MR. TUMULTY (*His Secretary*).

A GRACIOUS PRESENCE.

AN ATTENDANT.

The Instrument

SCENE : *Washington. March 4th, 1921.*

*Through the large windows of this rather stiffly
composed sitting-room Washington conveys an
ample and not unimpressive view of its official
character. The distant architecture, rising out
of trees, is almost beautiful, and would be quite,
if only it could manage to look a little less self-
satisfied and prosperous. Outside is a jubilant
spring day ; inside something which much more
resembles the wintering of autumn. For though
this is an entry over which the door has just
opened and closed, it is in fact an exit, final and
complete, from the stage of world-politics, made
by one who in his day occupied a commanding
position of authority and power. That day is now
over. In the distance an occasional blare of brass
and the beat of drums tells that processions are still
moving through the streets of the capital, celebrating
the inauguration of the new President. It is the
kind of noise which America knows how to make ;
a sound of triumph insistent and strained, having
in it no beauty and no joy.*

The Ex-President moves slowly across the room, bear-

71

ing heavily to one side upon his stick, to the other upon the proudly protecting arm of his friend, Mr. Secretary Tumulty. Into the first comfortable chair that offers he lets himself down by slow and painful degrees, lays his stick carefully aside, then begins very deliberately to pull off his gloves. When that is done, only then allowing himself complete relaxation, he sinks back in his chair, and in a voice of resigned weariness speaks.

EX-PRES.   So . . . that's over !

TUMULTY.   It hasn't tired you too much, I hope ?

EX-PRES.   Too much for what, my dear Tumulty ? I've time to be tired now.   What else, except to be tired, is there left for me to do ?

TUMULTY.   Obey doctor's orders.

EX-PRES.   He let me go.

TUMULTY (*shrewdly*).   You would have gone in any case.

EX-PRES.   Yes.

   (*Tumulty adjusts the cushions at his back.*)
Thank you.

TUMULTY (*seating himself*).   Well, Governor, now you've seen him in place, what do you think of him ?

EX-PRES.   Oh, I find him—quite—what I expected him to be.   I think he means well.

TUMULTY.   A new President always does.

72

EX-PRES. (*slowly pondering his words*). Yes . . . that's true . . . " means well."

TUMULTY (*tactfully providing diversion*). The big crowd outside was very friendly, I thought.

EX-PRES. Yes . . . couldn't have been friendlier. . . . It let me alone.

TUMULTY. Well, of course, they'd come mainly to see the new President.

EX-PRES. Of course. So had I. Yes, I believe Harding's a good man. He was very kind, very considerate. I feel grateful.

TUMULTY (*with rich emotion*). That's how a good many of us are feeling to you, Governor : to-day very specially. It's what I've come back to say.

EX-PRES. That's very good of you. We've had— differences of opinion ; but you've always been loyal.

TUMULTY. I think, President—— Forgive me ; the word slipped out.

EX-PRES. No matter.

TUMULTY. I think there's been more loyalty— at heart—than you know. Behind all our differences, in the party (as, with such big issues, couldn't be avoided)—well ; they didn't cut so deep as they seemed to. They were all proud of you, even though we couldn't always agree. Of course there've been exceptions.

O

EX-PRES. I don't want to judge the exceptions now (as perhaps I have done in the past) more hardly than I judge myself. . . . Tumulty, I've failed.

TUMULTY (*extenuatingly*). In a way—yes: for a time, no doubt.

EX-PRES. Absolutely.

TUMULTY. I don't agree.

EX-PRES. Because you don't know.

TUMULTY. Governor, I know a good deal.

EX-PRES. Oh, yes; you've been a right hand to me—all through. Others weren't. So I had to leave them alone, and—be alone. When I made that choice, it seemed not to matter : my case was so strong—and I had such faith in it ! It was that did for me !

TUMULTY. Chief, I'm not out to argue with you—to make you more tired than you are already. But if I don't say anything, please don't think I'm agreeing with you.

EX-PRES. I'm accustomed to people not agreeing with me, Tumulty. . . . Yes: too much faith—not in what I stood for, but in myself : perhaps—though there I'm not so sure—perhaps too little in others. To some I gave too much : and the mischief was done before I knew.

TUMULTY. You don't need to name him, President.

EX-PRES. I don't need to name anyone now. Some-

74

times a man may know his own points of weakness too well—guard against them to excess, be over-cautious because of them ; and then, trying to correct himself, just for once he's not cautious enough. But where I failed was in getting the loyalty and co-operation of those who didn't agree with me so thoroughly as you did. And I ought to have done it ; for that is a part of government. Your good executive is the man who gets all fish into his net. I failed : I caught some good men, but I let others go. There was fine material to my hand which I didn't recognise, or didn't use so well as I should have done. I hadn't the faculty of letting others think for me : when I tried, it went badly ; they didn't respond. So—I did all myself.

TUMULTY (*airing himself a little*). You always listened to *me*, Governor.

EX-PRES. Yes, Tumulty, yes. And you weren't offended when I—didn't pay any attention.

TUMULTY. When you *had* paid attention, you mean.

EX-PRES. Perhaps I do. My way of paying attention has struck others differently. They think I'm one who doesn't listen—who doesn't want to listen. It's a terrible thing, Tumulty, when one sees and knows the truth so absolutely, but cannot convince others. That's been my fate : to be so sure that I was right (I'm as sure of that now as ever) and yet to fail. Here—there—it has been always the same. I went over to Paris thinking to save the Peace : there came a point when I thought it was saved :

it would have been had the Senate backed me—it could have been done then. But when I put the case to which already we stood pledged, I convinced nobody. They did not want justice to be done.

TUMULTY. But you had a great following, Governor. You had a wonderful reception when you got to Paris.

EX-PRES. Yes: in London too. It seemed then as if people were only waiting to be led. But I'm talking of the politicians now. There was no room for conviction there; each must stick to his brief. That's what wrecked us. Not one—not one could I get to own that the right thing was the wise thing to do: that to be just and fear not was the real policy which would have saved Europe—and the world. . . . Look at it now! Step by step, their failure is coming home to them; but still it is only as failure that they see it—mere human inability to surmount insuperable difficulties: the greed, the folly, the injustice, the blindness, the cruelty of it they don't see. And the people don't teach it them. They can't. No nation—no victorious nation—has gotten it at heart to say, " We, too, have sinned." Lest such a thing should ever be said or thought, one of the terms of peace was to hand over all the blame; so, when the enemy signed the receipt of it, the rest were acquitted. And in that solemn farce the Allies found satisfaction! What a picture for posterity! And when they point and laugh, I shall be there with the rest. It's our self-righteousness has undone us, Tumulty; it's that which has made us blind and hard

76

—and dishonest : for there has been dishonesty too. Because we were exacting reparations for a great wrong, we didn't mind being unjust to the wrongdoer. And so, in Paris, we spent months, arguing, prevaricating, manœuvring, so as to pretend that none had had any share in bringing the evil about. When I spoke for considerate justice, there was no living force behind me in that council of the Nations. They wanted their revenge, and now they've got it : and look what it is costing them !

(*And then the door opens, and an Attendant enters, carrying a covered cup upon a tray. Upon this intrusion the Ex-President turns a little grimly ; but before he can speak, Tumulty interposes.*)

TUMULTY. You'll forgive this little interruption, Governor : I got domestic orders to see that you took it. . . . You will ?

(*The dictatorial expression softens : with a look of mild resignation the Ex-President touches the table for the tray to be set down. And when the Attendant has gone, he continues :*)

EX-PRES. No, they wouldn't believe me when I said that to be revengeful would cost more than to be forgiving. And still they won't believe that the trouble they are now in comes—not from the destructiveness of the War, but from their own destruction of the Peace. I had the truth in me ; but I failed. I was a voice crying into the void—a

77

President without a people to back me : a dictator—
of words ! And they knew that my time was short,
and that I had no power of appeal—because the
heart of my people was not with me ! If they had
any doubt before, the vote of the Senate told them.

TUMULTY. You said " the people," Governor ?

EX-PRES. The people's choice, Tumulty. The
vote *for* the Senate, and the vote *of* the Senate :
where's the difference ?

TUMULTY. Still, I don't think you know how many
were with you right through : and I'm not speaking
only of our own people. Over there it was your
stand gave hope to the best of them, so long as hope
was possible. But they were all so busy holding their
breath, maybe they didn't make noise enough.
Anyway—seems you didn't hear 'em.

EX-PRES. You can't reproach me with it,
Tumulty——

TUMULTY (*expostulant*). I'm not doing that, Governor !

EX-PRES. ——more than I reproach myself. If that
were true, then it was my business to know it. But
what I ought to have known I realised too late. When
I heard those shouting crowds—yes, then, for a while,
I thought it did mean—victory. But in the Conference at Versailles—Paris—I was in another world :
the shouting died out, and I was alone. . . . I hadn't
expected to be alone—in there, I mean. , I had
reckoned—was it wrong ?—on honour counting among

those in high places of authority for more than it did. We went in pledged up to the hilt : not in detail, not in legal terms, not as politicians, perhaps ; but as men of honour—speaking each for the honour of our own nation. And that wasn't enough ; for whom people stand pledged twice over—first in secret, then publicly—it's difficult to make them face where honour lies.

TUMULTY. You mean the secret treaties, Governor. That's been a puzzle to many of us : what you knew about them, I mean.

EX-PRES. Tumulty, I willed not to know them. Rumour of them reached me, of course. Had I then given them a hearing, I might have been charged with complicity, the silence which gave consent. Many were anxious that I should know of them—at a time when opposition would have been very difficult —premature, outside my province. And so—by not knowing—I was free : and when I stated the basis of the Peace terms, I stated them (and I was secure then in my power to do so) in terms which should in honour have made those secret treaties no longer tenable. There was my first great error—I acknowledge it, Tumulty : that I believed in honour.

TUMULTY (*reluctantly*). Yes . . . I see that. But it's the sort of thing one can only see after it has happened. You must have got a pretty deep-down insight into character, Governor, when you came to the top of things over there, to the top people, I mean.

EX-PRES. (*after a pause, reflectively*). Yes, it was

79

very interesting, when one got accustomed to it : highly selected humanity, representative of things— it was afraid of. There daily sat four of us—if one counts heads only ; but we were, in fact, six, or seven, or eight characters. And the characters sprang up and choked us. Patriots, statesmen ? oh yes ! but also " careerists." Men whose future depends on the popular vote can't always be themselves—at least, it seemed not ; for we should then have ceased to be " representative," and it was as representatives that we had come. And so one would sit and listen, and watch—one person, and two characters. Lloyd George, when his imagination was not swamped in self-satisfaction, was quite evangelical to listen to— sometimes. But there he was representative—not of principles, nor of those visionary sparks which he struck so easily and threw off like matches, but of a successful election cry for " hanging the Kaiser " and " making Germany pay." And having got his majority, he and his majority had become one. But for that, he might—he just might . . . yet who can tell ? That tied him. I was alone.

TUMULTY (*coming nobly to the rescue*). Then take this from me, Governor : for a man all alone you did wonders.

EX-PRES. I did my best ; but I failed. My first mistake was when I believed in honour ; my second, when I let them shut the doors. Yes, to that he got me to agree. Clever, clever ; that was his first win.

TUMULTY. Who, Governor ?

EX-PRES. (*with a dry laugh*). The man who told me he was on my side. The reason ?—a kindly means of saving faces for those whom he and I were going to " persuade "—of making the " climb-down " easier for them ! That seemed a helpful, charitable sort of reason, didn't it ? One it would have been hard to refuse. I didn't ; so the doors were shut to cover defeat and disappointment over the secret treaties. Then they had me : three against one ! And their weight told—quite apart from mere argument ; for each had behind him the popular voice (and when one lost it— you may remember—another came, and took his place). But against me the popular voice had shut its mouth : I, too, was an electioneer—a defeated one. Of my lease of power then, less than a year remained. After the Senate elections I was nothing. In Paris they knew it : and I could see in their eyes that they were glad. Yes, *he* was glad, too.

(*As he speaks, his head sinks in depression. There is a pause.*)

TUMULTY (*in his best sick-bed manner*). Governor, don't you think that you'd better rest now ?

EX-PRES. (*ignoring the remark*). And so the old secret diplomacy, balancing for power, with war as the only sure end of it, came back to life ; and I— pledged to its secrecies with the rest—I had to stay dumb. I was a drowning man, then, Tumulty— clutching at straws, till I became an adept at it. There, perhaps, as you say, I did do " wonders "—of a kind : all I could, anyway. That was my plight, while there in Paris we held high court, and banqueted, and drank healths from dead men's skulls. Did nobody guess—outside—what was going on? I gave one signal that I thought was plain enough, when I sent for the *George Washington* to bring me home again. But, though I listened for it then, there seemed no response. People were so busy, you say, holding their breath; and *that* I couldn't hear.

TUMULTY (*zealous, in a pause, to show his interest*). Well, Governor, well?

EX-PRES. And then, rather than let me so go and spoil the general effect (the one power still left to me!), they began to make concessions—concessions which, I see now, didn't amount to much; and so they persuaded me, and I stayed on, and signed my failure with the rest.

TUMULTY (*for a diversion pointing to the covered cup*). Pardon me, Governor, you must obey orders, you know. They are not mine.

EX-PRES. (*taking up the cup with a dry smile*). Executive authority has taught me that obeying orders is much simpler than giving them: you know when you've got them done. (*Removing the cover, he drains the cup and sets it down again.*) There! now let your conscience be at rest. (*After a pause he resumes:*) Tumulty, when I faced failure, when I knew that I had failed—— Yes; don't trouble to contradict me. I know, dear friend, I know that you don't agree; and, God bless you! I also know why. . . When I knew *that*, after the whole thing was over, and I was out again and free, do you suppose I wasn't tempted to go out and cry the truth (as some were expecting and wishing for it to be cried) in the ears of the whole world ?—let all know that I *had* failed, and so—that way at least—separate myself from the Evil Thing which there sat smiling at itself in its Hall of Mirrors—seeing no frustrate ghosts, no death's heads at that feast, as I saw them ? . . . I came out a haunted man—all the more because those I was amongst didn't believe in ghosts—not then. People who have been overwhelmingly victorious in a great war find that difficult. But they will—some day.

TUMULTY. Well, Governor, and supposing you had yielded to this " Temptation," as you call it, what's the proposition ?

EX-PRES. This . . . I had one power—one weapon, still left to me unimpaired : to speak the truth, the whole truth, and nothing but the truth, so help me God ! And the proposition is just this : whether to be stark honest, even against the apparent interests of the very cause you are out to plead, is not in the long run the surest way—if it be of God—to help it make good : - whether defeat, with the whole truth told, isn't better than defeat hidden away and disowned, in the hope that something may yet come of it. You may get a truer judgment that way in the end ; though at the time it may seem otherwise. Yes, I *was* tempted to cry it aloud—to make a clean breast of it—to say, " We, the Governments of the People, the Democracies, the Free Nations of the world, have failed—have lost the peace which we could have won, because we would not give up the things which we loved so much better—profit, revenge, our own too good opinion of ourselves, our own self-righteous judgment of others." . . . I was tempted to it; and yet it has been charged against me that I would not admit failure because I wanted to save my face.

TUMULTY. You have never been much scared by what people *said*, Governor. That didn't count, I reckon.

EX-PRES. No, Tumulty; but this did—that where all seemed dark, I still saw light. Down there, among the wreckage, something was left—an instrument of which I thought I saw the full future possibility more clearly than others. I believe I do still. And my main thought then was—how best to secure that one thing to which, half blindly, they had agreed. To win that, I was willing to give up my soul.

TUMULTY. It's the Covenant, you mean, Governor?

EX-PRES. Yes, the Covenant! That at least was won—seemed won—whatever else was lost. Some of them were willing to let me have it only because they themselves believed it would prove useless—just to save my face for all I had to give up in exchange. And so I—let them " save my face " for me; let them think that it was so—just to give this one thing its chance. And so, for that, and for that alone, I bound myself to the Treaty—stood pledged to do my utmost to see it through : a different thing, that, from telling the truth. Was I wrong, Tumulty —was I wrong ?

84

TUMULTY. No, no, Governor! You did everything a man could—under the circumstances.

EX-PRES. I have said that often to myself: and I hope, sometimes, that it may be true. But a man who gives up anything of the truth, as he sees it, for reasons however good—can he ever be sure of himself again? . . . It's a new thing for me to ask another man if I have done wrong. But that's the way I feel: I don't myself know. And once, once, I was so sure—that I was right, and that I should win!

> (*The situation has now become one which the friendly Tumulty would like to control, but cannot. As a " soul-stirring revelation of character " he finds it, no doubt, immensely interesting ; but to be thus made Father Confessor of the man whom he has followed with humble and dog-like devotion, knocks the bottom out of his world altogether. Moreover, he has received " domestic orders," and is not properly obeying them ; and so, dominated by the stronger will, he glances apprehensively, now and again, toward the door, hoping that it may open and bring relief, but himself sits and does nothing. Meanwhile, insistent and remorseless at self-examination, the Ex-President continues to wear himself out.*)

When a man comes really to himself, Tumulty—sees clearly within—does it help him toward seeing also what lies outside, beyond, and ahead—make him more sure that, as regards others, he has done right?. I don't know—I would give my life to know—if what I did, when all else had failed, was best. The political forces, prejudices, antagonisms, 'the powers of evil around me, have been so dubiously deceiving and dark, that I do not know now whether to have been uncompromisingly true to principle would have done any good. Perhaps after to-day I shall know better; perhaps only now have I become qualified to judge—a free man at last. Only in the secrecy of my own heart—now finally removed from all the interests, ambitions, fears, which gather about a man's public career—I do most earnestly and humbly pray that in this one thing I did right—not to discredit myself too utterly in the world's eyes, so that *that*, at least, might live.

TUMULTY (*doing his best*). It *will* live, Governor!

EX-PRES. It *may*. But in what hands have I had to leave it? To men who have no faith in it, to men who dislike it, to men who will try persistently, sedulously, day in, day out, to turn it back to their own selfish ends. There, in those hands, its fate will lie—perhaps for a generation to come. And it is only by faith in the common people, not in their politicians, that I dare look forward and hope that the instrument—blunt and one-sided though it be now—may yet become mighty and two-edged and sharp, a sword in the hand of a giant—of one whose balances are those of justice, not of power. But *I* shan't see it, Tumulty; it won't be in my day. If

America had come in, I should! That was the keystone of my policy: that gone, my policy has failed. That was my faith—is still; for faith can live on when policies lie dead. Think what it might have been! America, with that weapon to her hand, could have shaped the world's future, made it a democracy of free nations—image and superscription no longer Cæsar's—but Man's. That—that was what I saw!

TUMULTY. Perhaps they saw it too, Governor. If they did, it might help to explain matters.

EX-PRES. The Covenant was the instrument— and would have sufficed. So organised, America's voice in all future contentions would have been too strong, and just, and decisive to be gainsayed. Then life would have been in it, then it would have prospered and become mighty. It would have meant—within a generation from now—world-peace. Of that I had a sure sense: it would have come. To make that possible, what I had to yield to present jealousies, discords, blindness, was of no account—only look far enough! For there, in the future, was the instrument for correcting them—the people's vote for the first time internationally applied. And I had in me such faith that America, secure of her place in the world's councils, would have wrought to make justice international, and peace no longer a dream! Was I wrong, Tumulty, was I wrong?

TUMULTY (*expanding himself*). No man who believes in America as much as I do will ever say you were wrong, Governor.

EX-PRES. But when America stood out—when the Senate refused to ratify—then I *was* wrong. For then, what I had backed—all that remained then—was a thing of shreds and patches. Nobody can think worse of the Treaty than I do with America out of it, with the Covenant left the one-sided and precarious thing it now is. Had we only been in it—the rest wouldn't have mattered. Call it a dung-heap, if you like ; yet out of it would have sprung life. It may still ; but *I* shan't see it, Tumulty ; and that vision, which was then so clear, has become a doubt. Was I wrong—was I wrong to pretend that I had won anything worth winning ? Would it not have been better to say " I have failed " ?

TUMULTY. Forgive me, Governor : you are looking at things from a tired-out mind. That's not fair, you know.

EX-PRES. But if you knew, oh, if you knew against what odds I fought even to get that ! They knew that they had got me down ; and the only card left me at last was their own reluctance to let a discredited President go back to his own people and show them his empty hands, and tell them that he had failed. So a bargain was struck, and this one thing was given me, that peradventure it might have life—if I, for my part, would come back here and plead the ratification of the Treaty which they—and I—had made. Could I have done that with any effect, had I said that in almost everything I had failed ?

TUMULTY. Chief, I think you did right. But I

still feel I'm up a back street. How could things have come to fail as much as they did ? After all, it was a just war.

EX-PRES. Tumulty, I have been asking myself whether there can be such a thing as a " just war." There can be—please God !—there must be sometimes a just *cause* for war. When one sees great injustice done, sees it backed by the power of a blindly militarised nation, marching confidently to victory, then, if justice has any place in the affairs of men, there is sometimes just cause for war. But can there be— a just war ? I mean—when the will to war takes hold of a people—does it remain the same people ? Does war in its hands remain an instrument that can be justly used ? Can it be waged justly ? Can it be won justly ? Can it, having been won, make to a just peace ? No ! Something happens : there comes a change ; war in a people's mind drives justice out. . . . Can soldiers fight without " seeing red " —can a nation ? Not when nations have to fight on the tremendous scale of modern war. Then they are like those monstrous mechanisms of long-range destructiveness, which we so falsely call " weapons of precision," but which are in fact so horribly unprecise that, once let loose, we cannot know what lives of harmlessness, of innocence, of virtue, they are going to destroy. You find your range, you fix your elevation, you touch a button : you hear your gun go off. And over there, among the unarmed— the weak, the defenceless, the infirm—it has done— what ? Singled out for destruction what life or lives ;

ten, twenty, a hundred ?—you do not know. So
with nations, when once they have gone to war;
their imprecision becomes—horrible; though the
cause of your war may be just.

> (*Tumulty gives a profound nod, paying his
> chief the compliment of letting it be seen
> that he is causing him to think deeply.*)

That's what happened here. Do you remember,
did you realise, Tumulty, what a power my voice was
in the world—till we went in ?—that, because I had
the power to keep them back from war (for there my
constitutional prerogative was absolute), even my
opponents had to give weight to my words. They
were angry, impatient, but they had to obey. And,
because they could not help themselves, they accepted
point by point my building up of the justice of our
cause. They didn't care for justice; but I spoke
for the Nation then ; and, with justice as my one end,
I drove home my point. And then—we went in.
After that, justice became vengeance. When our
men went over the trenches, fighting with short arms,
"*Lusitania !*" was their cry : and they took few pri-
soners—you know that, Tumulty.

> (*Over that point the Ex-President pauses,
> though Tumulty sees no special reason
> why he should pause.*)

The *Lusitania* had been sunk, and still we had
not gone to war, and no crowds came to cry it madly
outside the White House as they might have done—
if that was how they felt then. The *Lusitania* lies
at the bottom of the sea. There are proposals for

salving her; but I think that there she will remain. The salving might tell too much.

TUMULTY. You mean that talk about fuse caps being on board might have been true? Would it matter now?

EX-PRES. Yes. It was a horrible thing in any case—disproportionate, like most other acts of war—and it did immeasurable harm to those who thought to benefit. But this—I still only guess—might do too much good—bring things a little nearer to proportion again, which the Treaty did not try to do. . . . What I've been realising these last two years is a terrible thing. You go to war, you get up to it from your knees—God driving you to it—unable, yes, unable to do else. Your will is to do right, your cause is just, you are a united nation, a people convinced, glad, selfless, with hearts heroic and clean. And then war takes hold of it, and it all changes under your eyes; you see the heart of your people becoming fouled, getting hard, self-righteous, revengeful. Your cause remains, in theory, what it was at the beginning; but it all goes to the Devil. And the Devil makes on it a pile that he can make no otherwise—because of the virtue that is in it, the love, the beauty, the hero-ism, the giving-up of so much that man's heart desires. That's where he scores! Look at all that valiance, that beauty of life gone out to perish for a cause it knows to be right; think of the generosity of that giving by the young men; think of the faithful courage of the women who steel themselves to let them go; think of the increase of spirit and selflessness which everywhere rises to meet the claim. All over the land which goes to war that is happening (and in the enemy's land it is the same), making war a sacred and a holy thing. ˋAnd having got it so sanctified, then the Devil can do with it almost what he likes. That's what he has done, Tumulty. If angels led horses by the bridle at the Marne (as a pious legend tells), at Versailles the Devil had his muzzled oxen treading out the corn. And of those—I was one! Yes; war muzzles you. You cannot tell the truth; if you did, it wouldn't be believed. And so, finally, comes peace; and over that, too, the Devil runs up his flag—cross-bones and a skull.

TUMULTY (*struggling in the narrow path between wrong and right*). But what else, Governor, is your remedy? We had to go to war; we were left with no choice in the matter.

EX-PRES. No, we *had* no choice. And what others had any choice?—what people, I mean? But that is what everyone—once we were at war—refused to remember. And so we cried "*Lusitania!*" against thousands of men who had no choice in the matter at all. Remedy? There's only one. Somehow we must get men to believe that Christ wasn't a mad idealist when He preached His Sermon on the Mount; that what He showed for the world's salvation then was not a sign only, but the very Instrument itself. We've got to make men see that there's something in human nature waiting to respond to a new law. There are two things breeding in the world—love and hatred ; breeding the one against the other. And there's fear making hatred breed fast, and there's fear making love breed slow. Even as things now are, it has managed—it has just managed to keep pace ; but only just. If men were not afraid—Love would win.

That, I've come to see, is the simple remedy ; but it's going to be the hardest thing to teach—because all the world is so much afraid.

(*And then, the worn, haggard man, having thus talked himself out, there enters by the benign intervention of Providence a Gracious Presence, more confident than he in her own ruling power. She moves quietly toward them, and her voice, when she speaks, is corrective of a situation she does not approve.*)

THE PRESENCE. Mr. Tumulty . . . my dear.

(*Resting her hands on the back of the Ex-President's chair, she surveys them benevolently but critically. Then her attention is directed to the covered cup standing on its tray.*)

Have you taken your——

EX-PRES. My medicine ? Yes. Your orders came through, and have been obeyed.

THE PRESENCE. It wasn't medicine. I made it myself.

EX-PRES. Then I beg its pardon—and yours.

THE PRESENCE. Will you please to remember that

93

your holiday began at twelve o'clock to-day ? I'm
not going to allow any overtime now.

EX-PRES. That settles it, then, Tumulty. And
that means you are to go. I had just been saying,
my dear, how much simpler it was to obey orders
than to give and to get them obeyed.

THE PRESENCE. Getting them obeyed is quite
simple. It is merely a matter of how you give them.

EX-PRES. You see, Tumulty—it's all a matter of
" how."

THE PRESENCE. There's someone waiting to speak
to you on the 'phone : wants to know how you are.
I thought I would come and see first.

EX-PRES. Who is it ?

THE PRESENCE (*indicating the receiver*). He's there.

> (*The Ex-President reaches out his hand,
> and Tumulty from an adjoining table
> gives him the instrument. As he listens,
> they stand watching him.*)

EX-PRES. Oh, yes. . . . That's very kind of him.
. . . Please will you tell the President, with my best
thanks, that I am greatly enjoying my holiday. . . .
Thank you. . . . Good-bye.

> (*He gives the instrument back to the waiting
> Tumulty.*)

TUMULTY (*with swelling bosom*). Governor, that
was a great answer !

EX-PRES. Easily said, Tumulty. But is it true ?

> (*But Tumulty's breast is such a platform for*

the generous emotions that he does no really care whether it is true or not. And therein, between himself and his hero, lies the difference. Grasping his fallen leader forcefully by the hand and murmuring his adieux in a voice of nobly controlled emotion, he obeys the waiting eye of the Gracious Presence, and goes. And as she sees him serenely to the door, the Ex-President looks ruefully at his painfully oversqueezed hand, and begins rubbing it softly. Even the touch of a friend sometimes hurts.)

(The door closes: the two are alone. She who-must-be-obeyed stands looking at him with a benevolent eye.)

PRINTED BY BUTLER AND TANNER LTD., FROME AND LONDON

A LIST OF VOLUMES ISSUED IN THE TRAVELLERS' LIBRARY

LONDON

JONATHAN CAPE THIRTY BEDFORD SQUARE

THE TRAVELLERS' LIBRARY

★

A series of copyright books in all branches of literature, biography, belles lettres, fiction, etc., designed primarily for the pocket or kit-bag, but also for the small house where shelf space is scarce and where two small books are more welcome than one large one.

Though the volumes measure only 7 inches by $4\frac{3}{4}$ inches, the page is arranged so that the margins are not unreasonably curtailed nor legibility sacrificed. The books are of a uniform thickness—$\frac{5}{8}$ inch—irrespective of the number of pages, and the paper, which is specially manufactured for the series, is remarkably opaque, even when it is thinnest.

A semi-flexible form of binding has been adopted, as a safeguard against the damage inevitable associated with hasty packing. The cloth is made specially for the purpose and is of a particularly attractive shade of blue. The binding has the author's name and the mark of the series stamped in gold on the back.

Each volume costs 3s. 6d. net (postage 3d.)

★

LONDON
JONATHAN CAPE THIRTY BEDFORD SQUARE

THE
AUTOBIOGRAPHY of a SUPER-TRAMP
by
W. H. Davies

¶ Mr. Davies is to-day a poet of established reputation, but his first, and until the publication of *Later Days*, his only volume of prose, has become one of the minor classics of the English language. Printed as it was written, without any academic corrections from the point of view of the Perfect Commercial Letter Writer, it is worth reading for its literary style alone. The author tells us with inimitable quiet modesty of how he begged and stole his way across America and through England and Wales, and how he lodged in prisons, in doss-houses and under the open sky until his travelling days were cut short by losing his right foot while attempting to 'jump' a train.

With a preface by G. Bernard Shaw

EARLHAM
by
Percy Lubbock

¶ 'The book seems too intimate to be reviewed. We want to be allowed to read it, and to dream over it, and keep silence about it. His judgment is perfect, his humour is true and ready; his touch light and prim; his prose is exact and clean and full of music.' *Times*

'He is in the front rank of living prose artists. If this has not been said before, I take the liberty to say it now, and to invite an examination of my claim which I am ready to rest upon a passage from any chapter of *Earlham*.' *Sir Edmund Gosse*

'The book is the romance of the impressions which grew in the mind of a child and were embalmed there, now lovingly disinterred and summoned to new life by the magic power of art.' *Manchester Guardian*

SELECTED PREJUDICES

Essays by

H. L. Mencken

¶ 'He is exactly the kind of man we are needing, an iconoclast, a scoffer at ideals, a critic with whips and scorpions who does not hesitate to deal with literary, social and political humbugs in the one slashing fashion.' *English Review*

'I recommend Mr. Mencken to any one who wants to read honest opinions fearlessly expressed.' *Punch*

'Reckoning must be taken of Mr. Mencken's supreme craftsmanship. No one like him for pointing his barb with the finest wit, dipping it in the subtlest malice, and feathering it gracefully with iridescent modernity. He is a perfect artist.'
Manchester Guardian

THE BLACK DOG

Stories by

A. E. Coppard

¶ A volume of short stories. 'Style knowledge of character, originality of theme and method—Mr. Coppard has them all. A remarkable writer.' *Saturday Review*

'Mr. Coppard is a born story-teller. The book is filled with a variety of delightful stuff: no one who is interested in good writing in general, and good short stories in particular, should miss it.' *Spectator*

'Mr. Coppard has many great gifts as a writer of short stories; and *The Black Dog* deserves a circulation far greater than that attained by most popular novels. Altogether this is a most unusual and entertaining book.' *Westminster Gazette*

WIDE SEAS & MANY LANDS

A Personal Narrative by

Arthur Mason

¶ ' It sometimes happens that the writer who really has something to say, is, by nature, a born writer. He finds to his surprise that it is as easy to tell his story as it was to live it. We have the feeling that we are face to face with the touch, the magic touch, of reality, and with the authentic glamour of a real and not imaginary past. . . . Mr. Mason's book makes the sea and all that belongs to the sea and ships live for the most dusty, dried-up, stay-at-home, prosaic, city-bound, inadventurous land-lubber.' *From the Introduction by* MAURICE BARING

' A book which the reader will be glad to have taken up and of which he will not skip a page.' *Glasgow Herald*

CAN SUCH THINGS BE?

by

Ambrose Bierce

¶ A collection of tales of mystery and adventure including :

<table>
<tr><td>THE DEATH OF HALPIN FRAYSER</td><td>A BABY TRAMP</td></tr>
<tr><td>THE SECRET OF MACARGER'S GULCH</td><td>THE NIGHT-DOINGS AT 'DEADMAN'S'</td></tr>
<tr><td>ONE SUMMER NIGHT</td><td>BEYOND THE WALL</td></tr>
<tr><td>THE MOONLIT ROAD</td><td>A PSYCHOLOGICAL WRECKSHIP</td></tr>
<tr><td>A DIAGNOSIS OF DEATH</td><td>THE MIDDLE TOE OF THE RIGHT FOOT</td></tr>
<tr><td>MOXON'S MASTER</td><td>JOHN MORTONSON'S FUNERAL</td></tr>
<tr><td>A TOUGH TUSSLE</td><td>THE REALM OF THE UNREAL</td></tr>
<tr><td>ONE OF TWINS</td><td>JOHN BARTINE'S WATCH</td></tr>
<tr><td>THE HAUNTED VALLEY</td><td>THE DAMNED THING</td></tr>
<tr><td>A JUG OF SYRUP</td><td>HAÏTA THE SHEPHERD</td></tr>
<tr><td>STALEY FLEMING'S HALLUCINATIONS</td><td>AN INHABITANT OF CARCOSA</td></tr>
<tr><td>A RESUMED IDENTITY</td><td>THE STRANGER</td></tr>
</table>

BABBITT

A Novel by

Sinclair Lewis

¶ 'Mr. Sinclair Lewis's masterly study.' *The Times*

'This extraordinarily penetrating account of the ordinary man.'
Yorkshire Post

'A tremendous book.' *Evening News*

'*Babbitt* is a triumph.' *Hugh Walpole*

'One of the greatest novels I have read for a long time.'
H. G. Wells

'His work has that something extra, over and above, which makes
the work of art, and it is signed in every line with the unique
personality of the author.' *Rebecca West*

THE DREAM

A Novel by

H. G. Wells

¶ *The Dream* is one of the most characteristic books that Mr. Wells
has written. The idea of telling a story of to-day from the
standpoint of two thousand years hence gives a delightful fresh-
ness to familiar things, and the two love stories are among the
best Mr. Wells has devised.

'It is the richest, most generous and absorbing thing that Mr.
Wells has given us for years and years.' *Daily News*

'I find this book as close to being magnificent as any book that
I have ever read. It is full of inspiration and life.'
Daily Graphic

'*The Dream* is a great book, one of the greatest, that Mr. Wells
has written, and it is most gloriously amusing.' *Everywoman*

EREWHON

A Satire by

Samuel Butler

¶ ' To lash the age, to ridicule vain pretension, to expose hypocrisy, to deride humbug in education, politics and religion, are tasks beyond most men's powers; but occasionally, very occasionally, a bit of genuine satire secures for itself more than a passing nod of recognition. *Erewhon*, I think, is such a satire. . . . The best of its kind since *Gulliver's Travels*.' *Augustine Birrell*

' *Erewhon* is very nearly the finest of satires.' *H. W. Nevison*

' If you do not know *Erewhon* you have a treat in store. The brilliant satire is amazing, and the Erewhonians should be as familiar to every student of literature as the Bobdingnagians.'
Sphere

THE MIND IN THE MAKING

An Essay by

James Harvey Robinson

¶ ' For me, I think James Harvey Robinson is going to be almost as important as was Huxley in my adolescence, and William James in later years. It is a cardinal book. I question whether in the long run people may not come to it, and the school of social research associated with it, as making a new initiative into the world's thought and methods.' *From the Introduction by*
H. G. WELLS

' A book for youth; yet older people, with some courage to face the evils of our present state, will find it curiously exhiliarating.'
Manchester Guardian

THE CRAFT OF FICTION

by

Percy Lubbock

¶ 'One of the most remarkable and fruitful books of criticism written in recent years.' *The London Mercury*

'As a plea for better reading his book is invaluable.'
Manchester Guardian

'A model of all that such a treatise should be.' *Nation*

'No more substantial or more charming volume of criticism has been published in our time.' *Observer*

'To say that this is the best book on the subject is probably true ; but it is more to the point to say that it is the only one.'
Times Literary Supplement

THE WAY OF ALL FLESH

A Novel by

Samuel Butler

¶ 'After reading it we hardly care to inspect some of the master-pieces of English Fiction ; it would be as unkind as to let in the cold light of day upon a dowager in a ball dress. Forget your connoisseurship . . . and you will find *The Way of All Flesh* the more interesting the more you read it.' *The Times*

'It drives one almost to despair of English Literature when one sees so extraordinary a study of English life as Butler's posthumous *Way of All Flesh* making so little impression. Really, the English do not deserve to have great men.' *George Bernard Shaw*

EREWHON REVISITED

A Satire by

Samuel Butler

¶ 'There are passages in it that rank among the best examples of plain prose in the language.' *Bookman*

'He waged a sleepless war with the mental torpor of the prosperous, complacent England around him, and he brought into the field a rarely paralleled versatility of talent and resource; a Swift with the soul of music in him, and completely sane; a liberator of humanity operating with the wit and malice and coolness of Mephistopheles.' *Manchester Guardian*

ANGELS & MINISTERS, AND OTHER PLAYS

by

Laurence Housman

Imaginary portraits of political characters done in dialogue— Queen Victoria, Disraeli, Gladstone, Parnell, Joseph Chamberlain, and Woodrow Wilson.

¶ 'Mr. Housman in this exquisite little book lends a delicate hand in the contemporary determination to gild the age. . . . He has the quality—to see ridicule in a beloved object without loving the object the less. . . . These eminent Victorians are transfixed in typical attitudes.' *Manchester Guardian*

'It is all so good that one is tempted to congratulate Mr. Housman on a true masterpiece.' *Times*

THE CONQUERED

by

Naomi Mitchison

A Story of the Gauls under Cæsar

¶ 'With *The Conquered* Mrs. Mitchison establishes herself as the best, if not the only, English historical novelist now writing. It seems to me in many respects the most attractive and poignant historical novel that I have ever read.' *New Statesman*

'*The Conquered* is a peculiarly fascinating work. If on themes less immediately attractive to her, Mrs. Mitchison can labour with the same rare union of simplicity and insight, she is assured of an especial position among modern novelists.' *The Outlook*

'She has, as it were by miracle, got back into the air and mood of the time she writes about: she creates and recreates. The splendour and mystery come easy to her; she is at home.' *Saturday Review*

'There is no criticism to be offered about this book. We can only say we think it one of the best historical novels we have read.' *Spectator*

'*The Conquered* is not only a fascinating example of the art of story telling, it is the sort of book that makes for better understanding by men of other men.' *Time and Tide*

★

LONDON

JONATHAN CAPE THIRTY BEDFORD SQUARE

JONATHAN CAPE LTD., PUBLISHERS
THIRTY BEDFORD SQUARE
LONDON, W.C. 1

★